# Self-Help 2.0

A NEW AND IMPROVED PATH TO
BREAK FREE FROM STRESS, ANGER,
AND CODEPENDENCY

To Gay,
Looking forward to
transforming this book
into workbooks.
Enjoy!

# Praise for *Self-Help 2.0* and the Pondera Process®

"I am beyond thrilled to have read this book, not only have I had the honor of having a few one-on-one sessions with Larry Burton, but now I have a guide and a constant reminder of how I can use this book to overcome the pain, the hurt, the fear, the frustration, and how to heal myself with the Pondera Process.

I have been through quite a journey, from my Grandparents passing to my own insecurities and limiting beliefs, that I was having a really hard time forgiving those who had hurt me as a child, and it was really affecting my day-to-day life because I didn't realize I had not forgiven them and believed I was not good enough. But now I realized they did the best they could and am healing using the Pondera Process to forgive, have compassion, and have unconditional love for myself so I can heal my heart and soul.

As you read this book keep an open mind and an open heart. There is a lot of great information, so be kind and patient with yourself when you start doing the Pondera Process. I truly believe that this book will make a great impact for those who are ready to let go of fear, to let go of the hurt, and overcome all your insecurities so you can accomplish your life goals or live a happier healthier life. Many thanks to Larry for creating such an amazing technique to help us learn how to heal with the Pondera Process."

**Rocio P.**

"I have used the Pondera Process to address a number of issues in my life, but certainly the most dramatic results issued from the process to diffuse old resentments. One tenacious frustration going back some forty years concerned my loaning a valuable item to a person who not only lost it, but then resented my holding him accountable. The other more recently involved a parson who misused his considerable authority in such a way as to cause a huge rift in a cherished organization. I simply could not think of either of these individuals without seething. I could not let them go; the personal pain was too deep. It was most discouraging.

Then I subjected each individual to the Pondera Process, and it truly was as if a large burden had been lifted off my chest. I remember sitting in my chair after having dealt with the first individual, and feeling a kind of freedom from years of bondage. I could bring up the person's image in my mind without triggering the anger, frustration, and resentment that had been present for so long.

The following week I handled the second individual using the Pondera Process. Same enlightening result.

It is a great gift to me to be out from under the emotional blackmail of those two individuals (neither of whom was aware of my anger, I'm sure). Although I had struggled on my own to forgive them and move on, I had been unsuccessful, and that in itself was most frustrating. But now I am free. Thank you, Pondera Process."

**Paul K.**

"Four years ago, I developed a rare, very painful, autoimmune disease. At that point in my life, I was experiencing many unrecognized (by me) stressors which quite possibly triggered the disease.

Six months later, Larry was recommended to me. I was very doubtful that he could help, but I trusted the person who made the recommendation. We began FaceTime counseling and training sessions. With Larry's guidance, I looked at deep seated issues in my life, my responses to people, and acceptance issues. By going through various components of the Pondera Process daily, my life began to refocus. My relationship with God was strengthened as every breath in and out became prayers for healing, of praise, of thanksgiving. Friends commented on how much happier & calmer I appeared to be.

While Pondera did not cure me, Larry has given me coping mechanisms which enabled me to lessen the pain and discomfort and live a more normal life with less severe attacks. Pondera is still working for me today when the inevitable stresses of life occur.

Thanks Larry, for teaching me I don't have to be everything to everybody!"

**Becky S.**

"Before using the Pondera Process, I was emotionally bankrupt. I'm a recovering addict and had been working in the field of addiction for 25 years at the same place I gained the tools and a better understanding of my addiction. I was comfortable working in this environment and loved watching women transform their lives. But when I lost my job of 25 years, I lost my self-worth and self-esteem, I felt as if my life was over and I no longer had a purpose or reason to live. Funny thing is that I did not want to use drugs or drink, but I contemplated many thoughts of suicide by running my car off a cliff. I felt like a lost soul that was just existing and occupying space on this earth. Somehow, someone which I choose to call "God my Divine" led me to Larry and group of loving individuals that were processing their life experiences through the Pondera Process. I began to implement the Pondera Process in my daily morning meditation and joined the circle on a weekly basis.

While using the Pondera Process, I had a breakthrough "a spiritual awakening" that made me realize I was a genuine, loving and caring person that has a lot to offer others. I realized that my story of recovery was powerful and my story of falling down financially after losing my job could help many. I began to feel worthy once again and began to fill my soul with life, I began to feel that I could love others once again and allowed myself to open up and prepare myself to receive the love of others. All I wanted was to feel alive and worthy.

As a result of using the Pondera Process, I began to feel worthy and alive. I began to feel God in my life again ... I never stopped believing in God, but I did not feel His presence during my moments of despair, and I could feel Him stronger than ever around me. I could hear Him whispering to me telling me everything was going to be ok and that things would get better. Gradually, my life began to come together, not exactly the way I wanted it to, but the way God felt was best for me. The Pondera Process helped me to see my life differently, helped me to let go, let go of what served me no purpose, to let go of negative thoughts, to let go of negative individuals and past experiences. Once I was able to surrender and let go of all negativity and obstacles, I was able to allow good and positive energy and positive influences to flow freely into my life. I AM NO LONGER CRIPPLED BY MY PAST."

**Doreen G.**

"What appeals to me most about working with Larry is his emphasis on positive, practical results. For every problem that I've brought to him he's been able to help me find the underlying root of the issue and treat the cause, not just the symptoms. I now firmly believe that there is no challenge I face that can't be made easier to overcome with his help!"

**Colin B.**

"I've noticed a great deal more serenity in my life. My focus is on important things that I can accomplish with joy. I appreciate myself a lot more and I am a more grateful person. I have enriched and deepened my relationships."

**Bill D.**

"Following surgery for colon cancer and sepsis I became down and not caring about living. While using the Pondera Process I found my sadness lifting and my will to live returning. I also used the Pondera sadness for healing and the doctors were amazed at how rapidly I recovered.

As a result of using this Process for my initial problems, I have found that my outlook on life and living is more positive and I am able to help others. My attitude of gratitude has greatly improved. Thank you for showing me the Pondera Process."

**Madeline B.**

"Before using the Pondera Process, I was overwhelmed by life. I was consumed by my problems at work and felt very alone. My thinking was unclear and I was in need of perspective.

During my time with Larry and using the Pondera Process, I regained perspective. I recaptured my connection to God. I realized I was not alone and that I can draw strength from the Holy Spirit.

Life continues to be a journey filled with ups and downs. With the power of the Holy Spirit and my connection to this power through the Pondera Process I can once again enjoy life."

**Marzel N.**

"Before my introduction to the Pondera Process, life challenges could overwhelm me. So, I had a history of that, and self-inflicted pressure to get ahead also made things worse.

With the Pondera Process I began to learn how to make adjustments in my reactions to all sorts of situations, instead choosing to reach for spiritual peace and serenity.

With practice, I learned to embrace a calmer, more peaceful way of living, my well-being improving day by day. It has become a matter of working from peace and serenity, and then moving outward into the world. The greatest benefit was to realize that this experience was always there for me. It doesn't necessarily eliminate the bumps in life, but does allow me to be much more effective in looking after my emotional wellbeing. Now when things get tough, I know to step back, call up the Pondera Process and return to a quiet state that offers reassurance and peace."

**Hale A.**

"With energy work I have noticed that my positive outlook has increased. I have noticed that my gratitude towards the good things in my life has brought on more good things. I have noticed that my overall perspective has changed and caused me to no longer be at a standstill in my life/recovery."

**Christopher C.**

"My experience with Larry and energy work has been very surprising and rewarding. I have been using energy tools for over six months now and am sure it's helping me on several different levels.

My awareness of the energy flow in my body is something I never before experienced.

I whole heartedly believe anyone who tries it will have many positive outcomes.

Try it!! You will be glad you did."

**Bill M.**

"I have attempted recovery a number of times over the last 10 years. I only have 60 days sober, however this is the most peace and calm I have felt in a long time. Stress has always played a huge part in past relapses. And I believe energy work is the main reason I feel such a calm. I also know that due to the energy work, my mind is so much clearer with such a short time sober. It has helped me let go of things I thought impossible."

**John B.**

# Self-Help 2.0

A NEW AND IMPROVED PATH TO
BREAK FREE FROM STRESS, ANGER,
AND CODEPENDENCY

Larry H. Burton

ISBN # 978-1-7340849-0-0

Book Interior and E-book Design by Amit Dey | amitdey2528@gmail.com

Bonus Offer

FREE pdf of the Pondera Process®
for Loving Light

THE ULTIMATE SELF-HELP TOOL:
How to Help Yourself Feel Better in
10 Minutes or Less

This is for you if:

- You would like to become more centered and grounded
- You would like to feel a greater sense of peace and serenity
- You want to gain insight and clarity on how you can grow
  through a particular problem or challenge

Go to www.rebuildingafter.com
and get your FREE copy today!

To Eileen, a continuing example for the power of love being greater than any challenge this project, or life, can bring our way.

"If it's half as good as the half we've known, here's Hail! to the rest of the road." Sheldon Vanauken

# Table of Contents

# Please read the following important information

*T*he information presented in this book titled *Self-Help 2.0* ("Book"), including ideas, suggestions, processes, techniques, and other materials, is educational in nature and is provided only as general information. This Book is solely intended for the reader's own self-improvement and is not meant to be a substitute for medical or psychological treatment and does not replace the services of health care professionals.

This Book contains information regarding an innovative, non-medical/non-psychological technique identified as the Pondera Process® developed by the author as a self-help tool. The Pondera Process® is intended to help individuals reduce and/or eliminate limiting emotions, beliefs, and memories and to balance the energy around them. This balancing of the energy around any disruptive item is meant to bring greater clarity and serenity and is designed to make it easier for individuals to grow through and resolve whatever is challenging them. The prevailing premise of the Pondera Process® is that the flow and balance of the body's electromagnetic and more subtle energies are important for physical, spiritual, and emotional health, and for fostering well-being.

Although the Pondera Process® appears to have promising mental, emotional, spiritual, and physical health benefits, it has yet to be fully researched and therefore, is considered experimental. The reader agrees to assume and accept full responsibility for any and all risks associated with reading this Book and using the Pondera Process®. If the reader inadvertently experiences any emotional distress or physical discomfort using the Pondera Process®, the reader is advised to stop and to seek professional care, if appropriate.

Publishing of the information contained in this Book does not create a client-coach or any other type of professional relationship between the reader and the author. While the author has extensive experience as an alternative healing arts practitioner and life coach, the author is not a licensed health care provider. The author does not make any warranty, guarantee, or prediction regarding the outcome of an individual using the Pondera Process® for any particular pur- pose or issue. Further, the author accepts no responsibility or liability whatsoever for the use or misuse of the Pondera Process® by the reader.

By continuing to read this Book the reader agrees to forever, fully release, indemnify, and hold harmless, the author, and others associated with the publication of this Book from any claim or liability and for any damage or injury of whatsoever kind or nature that the reader may incur arising at any time out of, or in relation to, the reader's use of the information presented in this Book. If any court of law rules that any part of the Disclaimer is invalid, the Disclaimer stands as if those parts were struck out.

**ENJOY THE BOOK!**

# Introduction

The time has come for us to update our approach to self-help.

Today, the accumulation of research and the experience of thousands of people tells us that there is a better way forward. The traditional approaches to self-help have resulted in as much, or more, frustration as they have in tangible results.

There is hope. Indeed, there is new hope for self-help.

This book is my journey in finding my way past the frustrations and limitations of traditional self-help and embracing the benefits of enlightened self-help approaches. In this book I will share with you what I have learned and describe a more effective path which you can take to move through the problems and challenges of life, experiencing greater peace, serenity, and joy along the way.

Let me start by telling you a story. My story is unique, but it is not unusual. While the particulars are unique to me, the themes of my story will be familiar to you. It's a story of emotional pain and frustration that propelled me on a journey toward hope and serenity. Join me as I share with you my journey, the insights gained and the benefits received. May this book make your journey toward greater serenity a little quicker and a bit smoother.

It was 1954. My dad was 20 and my mom was 19 when I was born. My dad was already an alcoholic. Having lost his mother when he was nine years old and having been raised by his father and sister, both of whom were alcoholics, my dad learned early on to use beer as a way to cope with the stress and emotional turmoil of life.

It took 30 years for me to begin to understand how alcohol, or any addiction, can affect a family. It took another 10 years, a failed marriage, and twice being on the verge of a nervous breakdown, for me to realize how his addiction had impacted me and was causing problems in my life. Then it took another 10 years before I began to find a solution that has helped me to unwind the traits of an adult child of an alcoholic, and of codependency, that caused me distress and robbed me of my serenity.

Today, with another 14 years of study, experience, and coaching under my belt, I can truly say that serenity has become my normal emotional state. Nobody stays at one emotional state all the time. That would mean I had "flat lined" and I am not there yet. Instead, I accept that life is an emotional roller coaster, but the highs and lows are no longer as dramatic or persistent as they used to be. There is now a sense of peace and security that pervades my life which allows me to respond, rather than react, to the challenges of life.

Fortunately, there is a silver lining to the dark cloud of emotional turmoil that follows all of us who have been impacted by addiction. Because of my pain, and because of the knowledge I have acquired and the techniques I have learned during my healing journey - and because I am now experiencing increasing amounts of serenity in my life - I can share with you the hope and practical suggestions that can make your healing journey a bit smoother.

Despite my life experience, this book is not specifically about how to deal with the negative impact of addiction in your life. It is about something more fundamental. This book is about changing the way we see ourselves and how we look at the problems and challenges that every life encounters.

I am going to suggest that it's time we bring self-help into the 21st century. Scientific research has shown that the assumptions underlying traditional self-help are outdated and incomplete. We are also discovering ways to combine scientific understandings with timeless spiritual truths to create more empowering, more enlightened self-help approaches. The time has come to bring new hope to self-help.

## Building a Bridge

My goal, my hope, my intention for this book, is to build a bridge from the traditional way we have understood self-help toward a 21st century understanding of how we operate as human beings and a more complete understanding of the life challenges we face.

So, let me start by giving you a snapshot of my life story (so far) and how I came to learn what I will be sharing with you, and laying out what you can expect from this book.

I am the oldest of 4 children, with a spread of 5, 9, and 13 years between myself and my respective siblings. This meant two things. There was always a preschooler in the house; and I was to be the "big brother". I was to be the responsible one because my parents were busy with the younger children. Looking back, I can see that the seeds were planted early for the two of the biggest challenges I have had to grow through.

First is what I call a case of ODSR - an overdeveloped sense of responsibility. This is a belief that is guaranteed to destroy one's ability to set healthy interpersonal boundaries and to radically stunt one's capacity for self-care.

The second big challenge was a serious anger issue. Anger became the way I found emotional strength and protected myself. Anger gave me the illusion of power and a way to feel safer.

Mix in to our family structure my dad's drinking plus his own anger issues and you get a very combustible family dynamic. For me, family life became littered with emotional landmines where I had to learn how to "walk on eggshells". I never knew when I would hear a beer can being popped open and the uncertainty that followed that sound.

One consequence of this family dynamic, for me, was that it became very hard for me to trust or accept compliments. Allowing myself to feel "good" always ran the risk of having the rug pulled out from under me. I learned to keep my guard up and to be wary of the next emotional explosion. I learned to be emotionally numb which contributed directly to my twice being on the verge of a nervous breakdown.

Don't get me wrong, I remember lots of positive, happy, loving times in our family. But as with anyone else impacted by addiction, the joy always had a shadow over it. I could not risk letting my emotional guard down to feel completely safe.

At the age of 18, I was ready to escape my family living situation so I moved into a house with some friends. I kept working part time for a local construction company and driving for a delivery service. I also enrolled in college as a full-time student. Oh yeah, and the recreational use of drugs which had started in high school increased significantly. Within a year I was on the verge of a nervous break- down. I felt numb and normal life felt unmanageable. At this point, I knew that I needed a change of environment.

This was 1973, we were still in Vietnam, the draft went to a lottery system and the college deferment was eliminated. I drew a very low lottery number, meaning I would be one of the first to be drafted. The assumption at that time was that the government would start drafting people within a couple of years.

So, I joined the Air Force. I served 5 ½ years, saw a good piece of the world, and earned the education benefits that would allow me to finish college after being discharged. Those 5+ years gave me a chance to recover my old emotional self. I was still being affected by my ODSR and anger issues but I had a renewed desire to move ahead in my life.

In 1981, I married a woman I had met while in the Air Force. At the time, my gut told me that the marriage was a mistake, but my head said that I might never find another woman who would want to marry me. (Can you say "low self-esteem"?) I knew we had issues - her dad was also an alcoholic - but I figured we could work them out.

I would describe our marriage as tumultuous. My low self-esteem, and my inability to set boundaries or to care for myself emotionally, did not help. My anger issues and inability to feel safe emotionally did not help much, either. It was a marriage held together by a sense of responsibility rather than sustained mutual attraction. It was a marriage marked by poor communication, different values, and a feeling of emotional isolation. There was no shortage of resentment, a form of frozen anger, between us at the end.

The rocky emotional landscape of our marriage did not stop us from having 2 sons. They were and are a blessing, but at the time, their presence added rocket fuel to my ODSR and further suppressed any thought of self-care.

That marriage lasted about 11 years. By the end of it I had completely shut down emotionally because to feel meant to hurt. I did not want to be hurt, so I chose not to feel. I did not resort to drugs in order to cope. Instead, I again went to the verge of a nervous break- down, feeling numb and withdrawn and shutdown.

We decided to divorce in 1992. We had been seeing a counselor, individually and together for several months toward the end of the marriage. It was through that counselling that I first learned about codependency and the traits of being an adult child of an alcoholic (ACA).

Now, I had started reading self-help books during high school and had continued to read and study different books in the 25 years between high school and this part of my life. None of what I had learned or practiced had substantially helped me with my ongoing problems with anger, with my ODSR, or with the other various codependent traits I had acquired.

So, coming out of my first marriage I had the beginnings of an understanding about codependency and a growing awareness of the traits of being an ACA. I was motivated to find answers that worked. I didn't want to have to shut down emotionally in order to not hurt. I began to read even more voraciously. I desperately wanted to heal my soul and to address the aspects of my personality that were causing me problems.

I should mention that I had studied sociology and social work at a Christian liberal arts college. I was active in a church. Neither religion nor my understanding of the Divine at that time helped me with my immediate pain or the emotional challenges I faced. It would be another 10 years before I was introduced to information that made a radical difference in my well-being.

Fortunately, during those 10 years, I met an incredibly loving woman who took a liking to me. I had grown and healed to a point where I didn't feel desperate, I no longer felt as if no one else would want to marry me. Like me, she had been the responsible one in a codependent marriage and was actively learning and growing in order to enjoy a better type of relationship. We married in 1998 and the quality of our lives, individually and jointly, has consistently improved over the last 21 years.

While I had made incremental progress in my well-being after my divorce, I still had some deeper issues that caused me turmoil and limited my serenity. My ODSR and anger issues were not bad enough to blow up my new marriage but they definitely did not contribute to mutual bliss. The turning point for my starting to make noticeable progress on my ODSR and anger came in 2004 when I was introduced to neuro-linguistic programming (NLP) in a one-day sales training class. However, it wasn't this specific technique that made the big difference. My breakthrough came about when - in learning about the basis of NLP - I was introduced to quantum physics and the understanding that "everything is energy".

Stay with me here. I am not a "woo-woo" kind of guy. Instead, I see myself as more of a blue-collar spiritual person. I am open to and interested in anything that can make a practical difference in helping myself and others to realize greater serenity in life. I often describe my work as being a combination of scientific understandings, psychological insights and spiritual truths. I constantly try to increase my knowledge in those three areas and to translate what I learn into a practical application that can improve my/our well-being.

So, when I first heard the phrase "everything is energy" I was cautious. Then I learned what science has known for over 100 years through the work of Einstein and others that all mass (anything that looks physical) is a form of energy. What the training in NLP taught me is that having a greater understanding of the role energy has in our world and how to work with that energy can have positive, practical results for my/our well-being.

Since that initial shift in how I looked at and understood life and the emotional challenges we all face, I have made steady progress in realizing greater serenity in my life. Along the way I changed the phrase "everything is energy" to "everything is a form of energy". What I found is that all emotions, beliefs, and memories have an energy component to them the same way that matter is a form of energy. In addition, I found that learning how to shift the energy of emotions, etc., that caused me distress made a profound difference in the quality of my life.

But I'm getting ahead of myself here. Remember that the purpose of this book is to build a bridge so that you, too, can begin to see yourself and the challenges you face in a more empowering, constructive manner. This has been and continues to be both my personal and professional journey. The peace, joy, and serenity on the other side of this bridge make it well worth keeping an open mind and exploring this bridge.

Back to my story...

As I have shared, over the past 15 years, I have been actively studying, researching, practicing, and teaching how we can use current scientific understandings about the fundamental role of energy and our personal energy systems to more effectively help ourselves. It has made all the difference in my life and in the lives of hundreds of students and clients that I have helped.

My personal journey in learning about the diverse nature of energy in our world, about quantum physics, and about the field of energy psychology, actually started by "coincidence". As I mentioned, it started when I took a one-day sales training class in which I was introduced to NLP. I took to this NLP stuff like a duck to water.

I dove into the NLP training and ended up with an advanced certification in the field. I liked it because it was practical and it helped people in a practical way.

As I continued reading about this "energy thing" that was the basis for NLP, I came across a technique called the Emotional Freedom Technique (EFT). It struck me as being an even more user- friendly technique and equally effective, so I wanted to know more. That led me to a variety of workshops and trainings in the various ways that EFT can be used to help people. I continued to study the theory behind EFT, about working with energy, and about the practical application of this knowledge. In due course, I ended up with an advanced certification in this technique, as well.

As in any journey, each step leads to a new vantage point and new opportunities. My studies in EFT led me to the much larger field of energy psychology. It turns out that there is a national organization called the Association for Comprehensive Energy Psychology (ACEP) that is made up of licensed professionals and coaches, who are interested in blending our scientific understandings of energy with conventional psychology.

Well, it didn't take me long to become a member of ACEP. I was pleased to learn that they had an even more extensive training pro- gram on the theory and practice of using energy techniques to help people. You can guess what happened next. Naturally, I dove into their training program and became a Certified Energy Health Practitioner in 2012. Beyond the actual training, the greatest benefit was that I was now part of a group of people with similar interests, col- leagues who could continue to challenge my growth and expertise.

As part of my certification in ACEP, I was required to work with a mentor. To my good fortune, I was able to be mentored by Mary Sise.

Mary had collaborated on a book called "The Energy of Belief", which taught a technique called Touch and Breathe (TAB). This was significant because it gave me a broader understanding of how energy can take many different forms within each of our lives, and of how learning to work with energy in our particular life can be profoundly beneficial.

All during this time I had been teaching classes and working with clients on issues ranging from phobias to peak performance for athletes. However, more and more of my time was being spent working with people impacted by addiction - particularly people in recovery and people working through codependency issues. Given my personal history, this was a natural area of focus for me.

You can't work in the area of addiction and not encounter the 12 Step model. I read *Alcoholics Anonymous* a couple of times, along with other books on the 12 Steps. I was particularly impacted by the book *In the Realm of Hungry Ghosts* by Gabor Mate and his understanding of the dynamics underlying addiction. I began to consider how energy psychology fit in with these ideas. Looking at the 12 Steps also took me back to my philosophy and theology studies in college, and prompted me to wonder if all of these pieces fit together somehow.

The last ingredients to this stew of ideas and concepts were my exposure to the work of another colleague, Dr. John Diepold, and his Heart Assisted Therapy (HAT) technique. When I saw the way that John had simplified the process of working with our individual energy systems by focusing on the heart, another light bulb turned on for me. This was a way to make energy psychology even simpler, more practical, and user-friendly - all features that were valuable to me and my clients!

It was after being introduced to Dr. Diepold's work that the idea of the Pondera Process®, a technique I will introduce you to in this book, began to take shape. The Pondera Process® brings together the scientific understandings, psychological insights and spiritual truths from all I had studied and experienced over the last 14 years. The Process has evolved and developed over the last five years with the goal of making it as user friendly and effective as possible.

This Book is an attempt to pull together all of that study, research, personal experience and the experience of many others into a format that makes it easier for you to benefit from. You, too, should be able to enjoy the greater serenity that we have been experiencing!

## The Journey Forward

Let's take a look at how this book is laid out and what you can expect as you move forward through this journey.

Part 1 of this book provides a historical context for understanding the traditional approach to self-help and asks, "Is it OK to change the way I look at some very fundamental ideas about how life works and how we practice self-help?"

We'll start by discovering that making a fundamental shift in how we see something familiar is not new to our time. History is full of examples and I will share a few of them with you. This will help you to see that changing the way we look at self-help is both safe and well worth considering.

Having seen that changing the way we look at self-help has historical precedent; we'll explore the assumptions behind traditional self-help. I will introduce you to dualism, a philosophical framework that has shaped how we understand traditional self-help and much more. Don't worry, I will share with you a simplified explanation so that no one is overwhelmed.

We will then explore in some depth how energy is a very real dynamic in all parts of our lives. I will offer different types of evidence to support the validity of looking at our world from an energy point of view. As I mentioned earlier, I am a blue-collar spiritual guy so this will be scientific evidence and an understanding on the role of energy for regular folks.

Combined, these three chapters will establish a foundation of current scientific understanding which supports the use of energy techniques and a more empowering approach to self-help.

Part 2 will take what we have looked at in the first part and make it a bit more practical. I will introduce you to the 2D and 3D Perception Diagrams. The 2D diagram will give you a graphic representation of how the dualism discussed in Part 1 operates and makes it easier to grasp how traditional self-help works in our life. The 3D diagram will make it easier to understand how an energy framework compares to the traditional framework. I will also introduce you to the Belief Tree, a model that has helped many of my students and clients to better understand what lies beneath unwanted feelings and behaviors. When you better understand why you feel and act the way you do, it is easier to make any desired changes.

In addition to providing graphic representations which can help make the concepts we are discussing more practical and understandable, I will offer some insights which I have gleaned from my studies in psychology, sociology, and other relevant fields, along with my many years of experience. I will share with you some of the insights and understanding I have learned about emotions, beliefs, and memories which have been instrumental in my moving beyond a traditional self-help approach and experiencing greater serenity.

In Part 3, I will introduce you to an energy technique I developed, the Pondera Process®, which takes a more enlightened and empowering approach to self-help and makes it both easy and practical to use in your life. The Pondera Process®, uses a scientific understanding of the human subtle energy system, psychological principles, and timeless spiritual truths to help people effectively reduce and/or eliminate limiting emotions, beliefs, and memories. This technique teaches you how to balance your energy around any behavior, emotion, belief, or memory which cause you distress. This balancing of the energy around a disruptive problem makes it easier for you to grow through and resolve that challenge.

The Pondera Process® can make it easier for you to begin making the changes you desire in a safe, easy way.

We will then use this new way of seeing self-help, along with the Belief Tree, and apply them to the challenge of stress. You will be provided with the necessary tools and learn a new way to approach an age-old challenge, gaining a more effective way of dealing with the stress in your life.

Having learned a more enlightened and empowering form of self-help, I will share with some thoughts on what self-growth can look like when using energy techniques like the Pondera Process®. I will pull from the writings of both social scientists and spiritual teachers to offer a transformation model which can guide your ongoing growth. You can think of it as a roadmap that tries to make a dynamic process a bit more objective and discernible.

In Chapter 9, I will use the content from Chapter 8 and share with you how I apply it in working with a typical client. I will give you some effective questions which will help you to see your path more clearly, and note some of the common obstacles encountered along the way (along with ways to move past those obstacles).

Finally, as a bonus, you will find the Appendix which contains material originally in Chapter 8. This is material that did not fit the flow of the book but was too good to leave out. The thoughts on energy Intelligence can especially be helpful as you grow into a more empowering understanding of yourself and of self-help.

With this book, I have tried to simplify some fairly in-depth content. In addition, after some of the chapters, I have included a "Resources" section with suggestions for those who desire to go deeper into the material.

Now that you have a sense of how I came to write this book and an overview of the book's content, let's start our journey toward a more empowering, 21st century understanding of self-help.

# A Note to the Reader

*I*f you would prefer to start with the content that can help you to feel better, then begin with Part 3 of this book. This content, by itself, is worth the price of this book.

After experiencing the benefits of the Pondera Process®, you can always go back to Parts 1 and 2 for an explanation of why it works. Bottom line, by moving from the traditional self-help approach which we have all been taught toward a more enlightened and empowering self-help approach, you can experience greater peace, serenity, clarity, and joy in your life now.

# Part 1

## Getting Started

# Chapter 1

# Choose a Paradigm, any Paradigm

When I started thinking about writing a book describing my journey from a traditional approach to self-help toward a more empowering form of self-help, my inner critic immediately jumped up and said, "Wait a minute!" I heard over and over in my head, "Who am I to challenge the status quo understanding of self-help?" After all, I don't have a bunch of degrees or licenses to make me an authority. Once I calmed that fear of not being "qualified", the next questions were more practical. "Where do I begin with this journey and how do I define the traditional understanding of self-help in a way that makes sense for the average person?

Let me take these questions one at a time.

Who am I to write this book? I am a fellow traveler whose life has been both blessed and challenged by taking literally Benjamin Franklin's admonition that, "It is the first responsibility of every citizen to question authority." The "question authority" part of the quote is a characteristic that has marked my personality since I was a toddler (that's what my mother tells me). I don't view the status quo as being something that is fixed or static, rather I see it as being dynamic and what we see as the status quo is just where the development of something has paused for a few years. I see the status quo as being something that needs to be updated, from time to time, when our understanding of something has significantly changed.

More specifically, I am a fellow traveler who has spent a lifetime navigating the emotional challenges of being alive. I have been on a continuous search for greater serenity in my life. What I have found is an understanding of self-help that provides a greater level of serenity and empowerment than the traditional approach to self-help provides. My hope is that by sharing my journey in this book, it will make your journey an easier and smoother one.

Next question, what is meant by a "traditional understanding of self-help"? The simple answer would be the way self-help has been taught for the last 100 years. The more substantial answer is to realize that self-help is just a system or methodology built on a frame- work of assumptions and ideas. This framework is referred to as a "paradigm", that is, the worldview underlying the methods used in traditional self-help. I will dive deeper into what that worldview is in the next chapter. For right now, the most important point is to understand that traditional self-help reflects a particular framework of ideas and assumptions about how people function and what they can do to help themselves.

But what if that framework is no longer accurate? Oftentimes, throughout history, it has been shown that the ideas and assumptions (the framework or paradigm) from a particular time in history are no longer accurate or true. Typically, it is an improvement in the scientific instruments being used and an accumulation of research that brings about our acceptance that we need to update the way we look at something. It is with that growing awareness, understanding and acceptance that any field or activity evolves and grows.

This is where we find ourselves today with our approach to self-help. Modern scientific instruments and the accumulation of research says it is time for us to update the way we look at our paradigm for self-help, to update the assumptions and viewpoints we have been taught.

Let me share a story to help illustrate what is meant by a paradigm.

Growing up, my grandparents loved to go fishing. During school breaks and summer vacations they would often invite me and my brothers to go along. They said it was to give my parents a break and to give us a treat, but I always thought they really just wanted someone to set up camp. Regardless, we loved to camp and fish, so it was a win for everyone.

One summer, when I was about 11 years old, I was exploring around the lake where we were camped and came across the skin of a large rattlesnake. How cool! Naturally I took it home with me and put it on the top shelf in the bedroom I shared with my brother.

Now, at this point in the story you need to know that my dad was afraid of snakes and wanted nothing to do with them. One evening, my dad came to our bedroom to say goodnight and casually rested his hand on the top shelf. He touched the rattlesnake skin, saw what it was, and nearly jumped out of his own skin!

My brother and I laughed so hard that we can still feel the glee when we remember our dad's reaction.

Once we stop laughing, an interesting question presents itself, why did my dad have such a strong reaction to a snakeskin while my brother and I didn't?

Think about your own family and friends. Why are you comfortable with an item or situation while others react to the same thing with anxiety? Why are so many people anxious about public speaking while some are not?

We know from psychology that it has to do with how we perceive, or see, an item or situation. Do we see the thing in question as being safe to us or as a threat? For whatever reason, my dad saw the snakeskin and it triggered a strong (and funny) reaction from him.

The way he saw a snakeskin, the way we see the world around us, the way we see self-help is called our paradigm.

## A Bit More About Paradigms...

Let me take a few paragraphs and share a bit more about paradigms and how there are numerous examples of them changing over time, throughout history. All of these changes through time shed light on the fact that the way we have come to view the traditional approach to self-help does not need to be set in stone. Our views on this can certainly benefit from a makeover.

According to the Oxford dictionary, a paradigm is "a typical example or pattern of something; a pattern or model." For our purposes, a paradigm is a pattern of beliefs, a lens through which we view and filter the world. For example, my dad saw a snakeskin as something to be afraid of, I did not. We each had a different paradigm, a different filter, through which we saw the snakeskin.

We all have paradigms, we're just not aware of them most of the time.

While the example of my dad illustrates how we each have our own individual paradigms/filters, groups of people also have prevailing paradigms or filters. I (along with many other fans) happen to enjoy watching baseball, while some of my friends find it incredibly boring. We see the sport differently. Or look at the differences in politics or religion. Different paradigms. Different ways of looking at the same thing.

In his book, *The Structure of Scientific Revolutions*, physicist and philosopher Thomas Kuhn described a paradigm as being a "set of received beliefs" which a community holds in common. He goes on to elaborate how science goes through a "paradigm shift" whenever it moves from one way of perceiving or seeing the world to another way of seeing the world, when it moves from one set of beliefs to another. In this book I am suggesting that the time for a paradigm shift in how we approach self-help has arrived.

## And Paradigm Shifts

Paradigms and paradigm shifts have been around as long as there have been humans. Whenever an individual or a group of people have decided to change what they believe about something, the way they see an item or situation, they change their paradigm.

In my journey, being aware that there are paradigms, and it is normal for them to change over time, made it easier for me to question the assumptions behind self-help as we typically know it. This familiarity with paradigm shifts made it easier for me to see that we are currently in the midst of just such a paradigm shift within the field of self-help.

We have paradigms/filters in all areas of our lives. We can't look at anything -- an object, a person, a social situation, etc. -- without looking through our individual or a collective set of beliefs. This includes how we look at self-help and the actions we can take to improve the quality of our lives, just as it goes for how we see a snakeskin.

Let me share with you some historical examples of paradigm shifts that have occurred on a large scale to give you some context. Shifts where society in general saw an old item in a new way and took on a new belief, a new paradigm. When you realize that paradigm shifts are a normal part of history and of progress then, like me, you will feel more comfortable looking at self-help with new eyes.

As you read through these examples, I would like you to note that there is a pattern to all of these shifts. In each example there is a combination of three elements which contributed to the paradigm shift:

1. A significant improvement in scientific instruments allowing individuals to see the world more fully and with greater clarity

2. The persistent and accumulated research of many individuals and

3. The passage of time.

It is helpful to see this pattern in the historical shifts of paradigms so we can better understand the changes happening today in the field of self-help. All three of these elements are present in the self-help field today. And there are exciting benefits for us when we become open to shifting the way we look at self-help.

But I am getting ahead of myself. Let's look at three historical examples of paradigm shifts and see what we can learn from them

## The Earth is the Center of the Solar System

We'll start with the saga of Copernicus, Galileo and their friends during the 15th and 16th centuries. During this time in history, the Catholic Church was considered the authority on all matters, including science, and it taught that the earth was the center of our solar system and all the other planets revolved around the earth. This way of seeing our solar system is known as the Ptolemaic or geocentric model of the solar system.

Then, along came Copernicus (1473-1543). In 1514, he started writing down his initial observations and thoughts. He came to believe that the planets of our solar system actually revolve around the sun. This model of our solar system is known as the heliocentric model. Copernicus continued to develop his ideas over the remainder of his life and published his findings just prior to his death.

Building on the work of Copernicus, Johannes Kepler (1571-1630) continued to research how the solar system operated and presented a model of the solar system which placed the sun as the focal point of our solar system and matched the observed planetary positions. Then in 1609, Galileo (1564-1642) built a small refracting telescope and began making even more refined astronomical observations. Many of Galileo's observations provided further support to the heliocentric model of Copernicus and Kepler.

Galileo then began to write about and teach this heliocentric model of our solar system. He used the accumulated research of those who came before him, his own research and the research of his contemporaries. Galileo continued teaching until the Catholic Church became very upset and started to crack down on him. For political and theological reasons, the church concluded that Galileo's writings contradicted the sense of Holy Scripture. Galileo's writings were subsequently banned and he was placed under house arrest for the latter part of his life.

On the heels of Galileo came Isaac Newton (1643-1727) who expanded on the work of Kepler and further confirmed that the planets of our solar system revolve around the sun.

Now, I've just simplified and outlined this brief history of how we see the solar system in a matter of minutes. Note that all three elements required for a paradigm shift came together during this period of history and enabled the Western world to change the way it saw the solar system. From Copernicus to Newton there was a steady improvement in the accuracy and power of scientific instruments, change came as a result of the cumulative research of many people and it took time. It is worthwhile to note that this paradigm shift, this change in our way of seeing our solar system, took over 150 years to become accepted and it faced a lot of resistance along the way.

## Atoms Have a Solid Nucleus

What is the book you are holding, or the electronic device you are using, made of? Up until the 19th century you would have received many different answers as there were a number of competing theories about the nature of matter. Today we take the concept of atoms as a given, but it was with the advances in science, in this case, the field of chemistry, before the concept of atoms was widely accepted.

Once there was general agreement on the existence of atoms, the next big questions were what does an atom look like, and how does it operate?

I recall being taught the basics of atoms in science classes in the 1960's. I remember models of an atom where electrons and protons orbited a nucleus in much the same way as planets orbit the sun. Perhaps you saw the same models.

And yet, scientists discovered in the first decade of the 20th century that the atom was actually made up of an electron cloud. Just as Einstein had discovered E=mc2, showing that mass/matter is made up of energy, so our model of the atom was further refined as we developed more powerful microscopes and gained a greater under- standing of atoms. Atoms are a form of energy.

Once again, the combination of improved scientific instruments, the accumulation of research and the passage of time equipped us to change the way we saw the atom. A paradigm that had existed for centuries shifted based on an improved under- standing of the atom.

This understanding that atoms, and hence all matter, are a form of energy, is a crucial insight that allows us to further refine and improve our paradigm for self-help. The paradigm behind self-help assumes that matter is solid, inert and has no energy dimension to it. But when we update that assumption with current scientific under- standings, the nature of self-help changes and the ability to help ourselves significantly improves. But more on that as we continue our journey.

## Genetics is the Whole Answer

This is a paradigm shift which is currently underway, happening during our lifetimes. As with the previous two examples, it is with the benefit of improved scientific instruments and the research of several individuals over time that our understanding is increasing and moving forward.

Our knowledge of genetics is based on the initial work of Gregor Mendel, published in 1865. His ideas were then taken up and further developed by William Bateson and his contemporaries at the turn of the 20th century.

However, our understanding of genetics took a significant leap forward in 1953 when James Watson and Francis Crick documented the structure of DNA as being a double-helix (you know, that shape that looks like two long worms crisscrossing themselves and making a series of oval shapes). Subsequent research discovered how DNA influences the behavior of cells, or what we call the genetic code. Then in 2003, scientists were successful in sequencing the human genome, that is, all of the genetic material inside of an organism. This is the understanding of genetics that the typical person has been taught.

Eureka! With this discovery scientists believed we had the genetic blueprint for human life and could solve lots of problems simply by altering an individual's DNA through medical interventions.

Not quite.

While advances were being made in understanding the physical processes within the cell, research was being quietly conducted by the cell biologist, Dr. Bruce Lipton, at Stanford University as well.

As he explained in his book, *The Biology of Belief*, Dr. Lipton "Realized that a cell's life is controlled by the physical and energetic environment and not by its genes." Genes are simply molecular blueprints used in the construction of cells, tissues, and organs. The environment serves as a "contractor" which reads and engages those genetic blueprints and is ultimately responsible for the character of a cell's life. It is a single cell's "awareness" of the environment, not its genes, which set into motion the mechanisms of life.

Thus, was born the field of epigenetics, "the study of the molecular mechanisms by which environment controls gene activity". The paradigm for understanding genetics had once again been shifted and improved.

The truth of this expanded understanding of genetics resonated with me personally when I considered the impact stress has on our physical well-being. We can measure the cortisol levels in our body and see how stress impacts our immune system and contributes to a whole host of physical ailments. And, when the person is removed from a stressful environment, their physical health typically improves. If genetics was only a physical process, as originally believed, then why did a stressful environment directly impact its behavior?

Part of the answer can come from Albert Szent-Györgyi, a Nobel Laureate in medicine, who said, "The cell is a machine driven by energy. It can be approached by studying matter, or by studying energy. In every culture and in every medical tradition before ours, healing was accomplished by moving energy."

Genetics assumed everything is matter and operates as a machine. Clearly that is not completely true and the paradigm of genetics needs to continue changing based on current research and as new scientific understandings are realized.

So, once again, an important paradigm is changing. The paradigm by which we see and understand genetics is being updated by further research and a willingness to challenge assumptions.

As you can see, the shift in paradigms, the shift in the way we look at familiar objects or processes has been changing throughout history and continues to change today.

Understanding the concept of paradigms made it easier for me to look at the traditional self-help techniques I had learned over the years and ask, what are the beliefs and assumptions behind them? What paradigm does traditional self-help use and does it need to shift?

## Resources

Thomas S. Kuhn, *The Structure of Scientific Revolutions* (University of Chicago Press; 3rd edition, 1996)

Bruce Lipton, Ph.D., *The Biology of Belief: Unleashing the Power of Consciousness, Matter, and Miracles* (Santa Rosa, CA: Mountain of Love/Elite Books, 2005)

# Chapter 2

# To Be, or Not to Be (Dualistic)

*T*hat is the question. I trust that Shakespeare will not mind if I adapt his famous quote from Hamlet.

So, what is the paradigm for self-help we have been taught? And is that paradigm an accurate understanding of how we as humans operate in light of the significant improvement in scientific instruments today, and the current accumulated scientific research and understandings?

Traditional self-help teaching is based on the dualistic, mind/body paradigm put forward by Rene Descartes and which has dominated Western culture since the 17th century. This paradigm for understanding human functioning says that everything flows from either the body, which operates like a machine, or from the mind/soul, which is the nonmaterial part of ourselves and gives us our emotions, etc. This two-part, or dualistic, paradigm has been fundamental to Western medicine, psychology, and many other fields for the past three centuries.

Think about your favorite self-help techniques. They probably focus on your doing something physical or something mental in order to help yourself. All of these techniques are based on a dualistic understanding of ourselves.

## A Closer Look at Self-Help

I have been a bit of a philosophy geek all my life. I really enjoy the history of how ideas originated, developed and show up in our lives today. So, when it came to looking at self-help and my frustration with the results I had been getting, it was natural for me to look at the ideas, the paradigm, behind traditional self-help.

I figured that when we have an understanding of the paradigm for traditional self-help teaching, we can then see if that paradigm is still accurate and true to what science is teaching us in our time. Just as people looked at the evidence and came to realize that the sun is actually the center of our solar system, so too can we evaluate and improve on the paradigm for traditional self-help.

Looking at the various examples in the previous chapter, we can see that it takes time and intention for a culture to change the way it looks at the world, much less the way it approaches self-help.

In order for us to grow and progress as individuals, we have to be intentional about looking at the beliefs we were raised with and ask ourselves if they still serve what is highest and best for us. Similarly, large groups of people need to be equally intentional and ask the same questions. Fortunately, we as individuals don't have as much resistance to change as the larger culture does. Resistance will always come from institutions, which have been built upon paradigms that can become outdated over time. These institutions try to keep us trapped in outdated thinking in order to maintain a financial gain for themselves or to maintain some form of power. However, we as individuals are free to use our intention and increased understanding to replace learned beliefs that no longer serve us, and as a growing number of individuals make this shift, a shift will inevitably occur in our culture as well.

So let's take a closer look at this paradigm for traditional self-help. To build a bridge from traditional self-help toward a 21st century understanding of self-help we have to know where we are starting from.

## A Bit of Backstory

Why did this paradigm - this way of seeing the world - develop? And, more importantly, has the advancement of scientific instruments, the research and experience of many people, and the passage of time, brought us to an inflection point where we would benefit from shifting our paradigm, shifting the way we look at the world, just as we have done on several other occasions over the centuries?

Now, a detailed look at the development of dualism is outside the scope and purpose of this book. Accordingly, I am going to limit our focus to one key element of dualism which we have assumed to be true and accurate, but which now appears to be an incomplete understanding of our world and of ourselves. We will lean on the excellent work of Richard Tarnas in *The Passion of the Western Mind: Understanding the Ideas That Have Shaped Our World View* as our guide.

Dualism has been around since at least early Greek culture. Our contemporary understanding of dualism was first developed and written down by Rene´ Descartes (1596-1650). Perhaps you have heard of his statement, "Cogito, ergo sum" or, "I think, therefore I am". That is a favorite catchphrase for Descartes. His writings are significant because his formulation of dualism has been a cornerstone of the Western worldview since the 17th century.

After the Roman Empire fell in 476 A.D., there was a vacuum created and people in areas previously controlled by Rome lost any sense of external authority and stability.

Into this gap stepped the Catholic Church.

The Church kept higher learning alive through its monasteries and provided a structure for civil society. The Church became a source of authority and provided a sense of identity and cultural unity to the people within its sphere. It also was seen as an authority in matters of science as well as matters of faith.

However, the dominance of the intellectual authority of the Church began to weaken during the Renaissance. People like Michelangelo (1475-1564) and Leonardo da Vinci (1452-1519) began to expand human capabilities in the arts and sciences. They did it while being respectful and in service to the Church, but they also became an example of man's ability to develop knowledge and understanding outside of the Church's teachings.

## Once Upon a Time, the Earth Was the Center of the Solar System

To illustrate this, let's revisit and expand on an example of a paradigm shift from the last chapter. In the 15th century, the Church taught that the earth was the center of our solar system and that all other planets orbited in a circle around the earth. While this understanding of cosmology had its origins in the work of Aristotle and was further developed by Ptolemy, the Church taught that this understanding of the earth's place was supported by scripture - that the Bible said it was so. The Church put itself into a position where being faithful to the Church meant you had to believe that the earth was the center of our solar system.

Now, along comes Copernicus (1473-1543) and he begins to challenge this central belief by showing that the observable movements in our solar system made more sense if the sun were the center of our solar system. This was significant because the authority of the Church was being challenged on the basis of reason, mathematics, and observation. Over the next 200 years, the work of Copernicus would be confirmed, expanded on, and solidified by the research of other people like Kepler (1571-1630), Galileo (1564-1642), and Newton (1643-1727).

By the time of Newton's death, the absolute authority of the Church in all matters, including an explanation of the natural world, could no longer be supported. Our solar system, indeed the entire universe, was now seen as a complex mechanical system. The paradigm had shifted to a belief that our solar system had been put into motion by God and all the planets revolved around the sun with predictable, mechanical precision.

## Then Came Descartes

When there are no longer central institutions or cultural traditions to govern what a culture believes and why it holds such beliefs, the result is an intellectual free-for-all with no agreed basis for a governing world view. Without an agreement as to what was true, and a basis for that agreement, culture becomes increasingly skeptical and relativistic. The discoveries by Copernicus and those that followed him, and the loss of absolute authority by the Church in all matters, resulted in an intellectual free-for-all.

Into this cultural/historical stew stepped Descartes (1596-1650).

Descartes was educated in the critical rationalism thinking of the Jesuits within the Catholic Church and he was exceptionally skilled as a mathematician. Seeing that the Church could no longer claim authority over an understanding of the natural world, and the confusion resulting from relativism and many competing philosophical traditions, Descartes sought to establish a new basis for absolute certainty. He wanted to protect the authority of the Church in the life of the individual while also freeing science to progress in the arena of the natural world.

Being a mathematician, Descartes believed he could use reason to establish a new basis for absolute certainty.

To accomplish his goal, Descartes proceeded to separate the world into two parts. The first was "res cogitans", which is Latin for "a thinking thing", as in the mind or soul. Being a "thinking thing" not only meant the ability to reason, but also included anything that has awareness or consciousness. This is what his maxim, "I think, therefore I am" is referencing. Descartes maintained that the ability to be a "thinking thing" is what set humans apart from the rest of nature. Second, Descartes then defined everything that was not thinking as "res extensa" or "extended thing" in Latin. This phrase was often translated as "corporeal substance" or what we would call mass/matter.

*It is in Descartes understanding of matter that things become interesting.*

Stay with me as I share a (very) brief explanation of this part of Descartes' thinking. I assure you that it is relevant to our finding new hope for self-help and building a bridge toward a more empowering paradigm. It is only in understanding his conception of matter that we can question if it is still a full and complete understanding of matter, or if current scientific discoveries require us to shift our understanding.

Remember, it is a dualistic (mind/body) worldview that is the foundation for Western medicine, psychology, self-help and virtually every other part of Western culture.

So, what was Descartes' understanding of matter?

Starting with the Renaissance and continuing through the time of Descartes, there was a renewed embracing of atomism – a conception of matter that was first put forward by ancient Greek philosophers. Atomism held that the universe was made of invisibly small "material particles (which) possessed neither purpose nor intelligence, but moved solely according to mechanical principles."

The philosophy of atomism fit in nicely with Descartes' "image of nature as an intricate impersonal machine ruled by mathematical law." This view of the universe as an intricate machine ruled by mathematical laws became the guiding paradigm of his time and continues to exert its influence today – despite shortcomings of this model that would be brought to light by Albert Einstein some 300 years later.

## Putting It All Together

The pieces were now in place for Descartes to put forward his philosophy of dualism. By combining his atomistic view of nature and the primacy of reason, to assert, "I think, therefore I am", Descartes drew a distinction between himself and everything not similar to himself.

Descartes started with *res cogitans* – a thinking thing - and added *res extensa* – an extended or material substance. In other words, he separated the human and their capacity for thought, awareness and consciousness from the rest of nature.

We can now summarize the paradigm Descartes put forth with this quote from Tarnas, "Thus *res cogitans* – thinking substance, subjective experience, spirit, consciousness, that which man perceives as within—was understood as fundamentally different and separate from *res extensa* – extended substance, the objective world, matter, physical body, plants and animals, the entire physical universe, everything that man perceives as outside his mind. Only in man did the two realities come together as mind and body. And both the cognitive capacity of human reason and the objective reality and order of the world found their common source in God."

In other words, Descartes said that there was "thinking substance, subjective experience, spirit, consciousness" (mind) and "the objective world, matter, physical body" (body). In addition, because of his atomistic view of nature, he said that matter does not have "awareness, purpose, or spirit."

**This last statement, the belief that matter does not have "awareness, purpose or spirit" is the weak point in dualism.**

It is Descartes' understanding of matter that is now brought into question by the current findings in quantum physics. All three elements which have led to paradigm shifts in the past are now present:

1. Improved scientific instruments

2. The accumulation of research by many individuals and

3. The passage of time

All of these elements require us to look anew at the assumed paradigm behind dualism and, thus, traditional self-help.

It is time for us to update Descartes' understanding of matter in light of current scientific discoveries, and to update the dualistic paradigm of the world which we have inherited. By moving from a dualistic understanding of the world, which we were taught and conditioned to believe, and moving toward a non-dualistic understanding we can have a basis for new hope. We can build a bridge toward a more empowering understanding of ourselves and discover new ways to solve old problems.

## Dualism and Self-help

Let me now come back to why this is important to us when we are simply trying to find a better way to help ourselves feel better.

The dualistic, mind/body paradigm put forward by Descartes has dominated Western culture since the 17th century and has defined the framework of self-help teaching. As I mentioned at the beginning of this chapter, take a look at all the self-help tools and techniques you have ever seen – probably 99% of them focus on the mind or the body. Techniques such as affirmations, positive thinking and vision boards focus on the mind (what you think), while techniques such as physical rewards, yoga and snapping a rubber band on your wrist when you have an unwanted thought focuses on the body (what we do). In addition, current day self-help teachings rely heavily on a treatment approach called Cognitive Behavior Therapy, an approach which specifically combines cognitive therapy (mind) and behavioral therapy (body). Dualism has clearly been assumed and has defined the traditional approach to self-help.

But what if dualism is not a complete description of our world or of ourselves? What if the atom is not inert matter, as Descartes believed, but rather has a quantum or energy reality to it? What if there is a more complete understanding of our world available to us and that understanding could unlock new ways for us to help ourselves?

All good questions. I wanted to find out.

# Resources

Richard Tarnas, *The Passion of the Western Mind: Understanding the Ideas That Have Shaped our World View*, (New York: Random House, 1991)

# Chapter 3

# Got Energy?

As I mentioned in the Introduction, the first time I had my dualistic view of the world challenged was 2004 when I took a class in Neuro Linguistic Programming. I had no clue what quantum physics was, much less how to approach my emotional challenges from an energy point of view. But if approaching my challenges from a new perspective could lead to greater serenity in my life, I was willing to listen and learn.

One of the first understandings that helped me, was to realize that my dualistic paradigm of the world (what I call a 2D paradigm) was something that I had inherited, not consciously chosen. By the same token, I had inherited a traditional approach to self-help. Let me expand on this point for a moment.

In my studies I came to realize that all of the beliefs we hold are learned. Think about it, babies aren't born with a set of beliefs. The way they see themselves, their family or their world is learned, and these learnings happen both consciously and unconsciously. For example, I can recall times in my life when I took on a particular belief, a particular point of view. Just as I can recall times when I consciously changed my belief about a particular item. But not all of my beliefs came from an active choice on my part, some of my beliefs were assumed. Some of my beliefs were taken on because everyone and everything in my environment told me "This is how it is". I took on beliefs in order to get along in my environment, whether that environment was my family, my community or my culture.

In fact, the dualistic or 2D paradigm we have used to look at the world up until this point in our lives is a paradigm we were given, not one we chose. We are free to question that assumed paradigm and ask if it is still the paradigm that is highest and best for us. Is it in our best interest to consider looking at the world from a different perspective in order to have a better quality of life?

This was an important understanding because it gave me the freedom to question what I had assumed to be true. It gave me the freedom to say to myself that it is OK that I looked at the world a particular way for 50 years because I didn't know anything different, and it was OK for me to change my paradigm now that I had new information.

I had to be able to let go of any self judgement for my old way of looking at the world. By realizing that all beliefs are learned, I was free to let go of beliefs that no longer served me and to take on new beliefs which would be more empowering.

Through gaining this understanding that all beliefs are learned, I gave myself permission to consider the evidence that there was more to reality than the 2D paradigm I had been taught.

So, what evidence do we have that tells us there is an energy dimension to life? That the 2D paradigm we were taught is incomplete?

When I started to outline this chapter of the book, I began by jotting down all of the different items I have seen, felt, and read over the last fourteen years which point toward the existence of an energy reality that underlies everything we sense and experience. I quickly realized that this chapter alone could be expanded into a couple of books. Indeed, a quick search provides over 1,400 book titles related to the energetic basis of our universe, with authors ranging from noted scientists to respected spiritual teachers like the Dalai Lama.

My desire in this chapter, then, is to provide you with a sampling of the range of evidence which supports the reality of energy as a very real dynamic in our personal lives and in nature. To do that without overwhelming you - or myself - I am going to note different categories of evidence that I am aware of and briefly expand on each one. I'll also provide some source material so that you can dive deeper into the research if you so choose.

Recall what I said earlier about the pattern behind paradigm shifts. Throughout history there has consistently been three elements present when a shift in a paradigm occurs: a combination of 1) improved scientific instruments; 2) the cumulative research of many people; and 3) the passage of time. In this chapter, I will intro duce you to the scientific breakthroughs and cumulative research that have been done in the area of energy which shows how it is fundamental to our world, and that each of us has a subtle energy system within us. Hopefully you will agree with me that enough time has passed that we can now embrace the energy reality of our lives and begin using that knowledge and understanding for our greater well-being.

## Overview

We each have an energy system. A what? They didn't teach this in my biology class!

I know. I didn't learn about this in my biology class either. A major reason for this lack of teaching about our subtle energy system is that science has been based on a dualistic paradigm and the existence of "subtle energy" doesn't fit into that paradigm. It is hard to see or acknowledge the presence of subtle energy when you have assumed and believe that it does not exist. You see, we didn't have the scientific instruments to measure subtle energy or to perform experiments which could prove its existence. But we now have the technology. It just takes a while for the education system to catch up.

By the way, knowledge of our body's subtle energy system has been around for at least 2,000 years. A lot longer than Western medicine. Acupuncture, a practice designed to promote the free and smooth flow of energy within your body, has been effectively used to promote physical health since at least 100 B.C. when the practice was documented in China.

Think about how your body is put together. You have a respiratory system which transports air throughout your body; a circulatory system that carries blood; an immune system that protects you. In the same way, your body has an energy system which allows energy to flow to and from every cell in your body. This energy flows along defined paths called meridians and tends to gather in 7 different focal points on your body - called chakras. This energy is often called "subtle energy" in order to differentiate it from physical energy, mental energy, or other forms of energy.

The energy in our bodies is designed to flow evenly and smoothly, like a gently flowing stream. However, when this energy flow becomes blocked, or scattered, we experience emotional distress and potentially physical ailments.

So how do we know this energy system exists and is a real dynamic in our lives?

Let me share with you seven different categories of evidence which support the reality of us each having an energy system which plays an important role in our well-being.

## Personal Experiences

Remember that time you met someone for the first time and felt an instant connection with them - or an instant feeling of caution? Or you walked into a room and something felt off? Or how about the time you followed a "hunch" and you were glad you did? All of these are examples of how we naturally pick up on the energy of a person, place, thought, opportunity, or other aspects in our life.

I recall the first time I "accidentally" met my wife of 20 years (and counting). We were both busy with careers and had dated all of the people our friends had introduced us to. It was the early 90's so we both decided to try video dating. Video dating back then required you to visit a central location, flip through binders of pictures with brief bios of each person and then look at a short video interview of those who interested you. It was pretty advanced technology for its time, kind of like video rental stores. She saw my video and wanted to meet me but I had not gotten her message yet. So, one Sunday we "happened" to be in the central location at the same time and she recognized me from my photo. When she came over and introduced herself there was a sense of connection and familiarity that went beyond all the people I had met before. I knew in my gut that this was a special person who I need to get to know better. Glad I did!

Now, these are completely subjective experiences and they don't carry much "scientific" weight, but they are real experiences nonetheless and indicate to us that there is more to the world than meets the eye.

Or think about how different types of music make you feel. Music is a form of energy and different types of music have a different energy to them, which affects our personal energy system differently and results in the creation of different feelings within us. We are able to see a sound wave, the unique energy signature of a sound, on instruments that measure the frequency and amplitude of sound. What we feel while listening to music is the energy signature of the music impacting our energy system resulting in a physical sensation. Consider what happens when a parent sings to their baby in order to calm them down. The baby doesn't know what the parent is saying or if they can carry a tune. They pick up on the positive, loving energy of the parent's voice and it helps to calm them. It is the positive energy coming from the parent and impacting the baby's energy system which creates the calming effect.

Or, how about the way different colors affect how you feel? There is a whole science behind color and its emotional impact.

When pure white light passes through a prism it separates into all of the visible colors, with each color having a single, unique wavelength. Similar to sound, light is a form of energy, so each color is a form of energy having an energy signature that shows up with its own unique wavelength.

Take, for example, the color green. Green is a restful color because it is in the middle of the light spectrum and doesn't require the eye to make any adjustment. It is the color of balance and the most dominant color in nature. That is not an accident.

It is the energy signature (wavelength) of the color impacting your energy system which contributes to the way you feel, with green tending to create a feeling of calmness. That's why performers wait in the "green room" prior to a performance.

## Near Death Experiences

Near Death Experiences (NDE's) are another area that show up in a wealth of literature. What has always fascinated me is not the particulars of any one story, but rather the common pattern of experiences, understandings, and teachings that individuals describe.

There are two NDE books in particular that spoke to me about the reality of an energetic dimension to life. The first was "Proof of Heaven: A Neurosurgeon's Journey into the Afterlife" by Eben Alexander, M.D. In it, Dr. Alexander writes about his experience of being in a coma for seven days, with that area of his brain which controls thought and emotion completely shut down. That a very rational neurosurgeon, with no belief in anything he could not see, would have a journey into realms beyond this world and live to tell about it, is very compelling.

The other book I would note is "My Stroke of Insight: A Brain Scientist's Personal Journey" by Jill Bolte Taylor, Ph.D. Dr. Taylor experienced a massive stroke at the age of 37 which shut down the left side - the rational/analytical side - of her brain. The book is the story of her experience of living from the intuitive right side of her brain and of her subsequent complete recovery. Here is a brain scientist providing a first-hand account of experiencing the reality that everything is a form of energy, and then her slowly regaining the use of the analytical portion of her brain. A very informative and inspiring story.

Again, science would say that these were subjective experiences that prove nothing. While they did not objectively prove to me the reality of our having an energy system, or there being an energy dimension to life, they sure proved that there was something going on that deserved further looking into.

## Power of Thoughts

Can what you think make you sick? Is it true that you can "worry yourself sick"?

Yes, you can.

We will get into this dynamic later in the book when we look at how our thoughts and beliefs connect to stress, which can lead to a weakened immune system, and make us more prone to illness in general. However, for the moment, I'd like to share with you an experiment which I have participated in, and which I have seen demonstrated several times in workshops. This demonstration shows the power of thoughts on the body.

Typically, a volunteer is chosen from the audience and is asked to stand at the front of the room with their back to the audience. The volunteer cannot see the audience or the presenter at this point. Next, the presenter instructs the audience to silently send out positive thoughts to the volunteer, such as "you are awesome" when they see the thumbs-up signal. Conversely, when the presenter gives the thumbs-down signal, the audience is to silently send out negative thoughts, such as "you are a loser".

The presenter will give the signal to the audience and then use muscle testing on the volunteer. Muscle testing is a simple process where you have a person stretch out their arm and you gently push down on the arm. Consistently, when a person focuses on a positive thought, their muscles will provide resistance to the downward push. When the person focuses on a negative thought, their muscles will become weaker and the arm will go down, with the same amount of downward pressure as before.

Back to the demonstration. The presenter has the volunteer close their eyes and then silently gives the audience the thumbs-up sign. Even though nothing has been verbalized, consistently the volunteer will "test strong" - their arm provides resistance. However, when the presenter gives the audience the thumbs-down sign, the volunteer's arm becomes weaker and provides little resistance.

It doesn't matter what sequence you use when giving the audience the thumbs-up/down signal. The effect on the volunteer is consistent. Again, nothing was said out loud. The most probable explanation for this phenomenon is that the volunteer is unconsciously picking up on the energy of the audience's thoughts and it shows up in their muscles becoming stronger or weaker, depending on whether the energy was positive or negative.

It's a fascinating demonstration, and I suspect that upon reflection you can think of similar times when you felt the unspoken and unseen emotion of another person. And it's just as true when we engage in negative self-talk. When we are negative, we compromise our physical well-being.

## New Tools, New Insights

Just as Galileo moved astronomy forward with his use of an improved telescope, so are we able to "see" the presence of energy through relatively new instruments. Let me give you a handful of examples.

If you have ever had your heart examined, then you probably had an EKG. What they were doing was checking the electrical activity in your heart. No electrical signal, no heartbeat, no more life.

Similarly, if you ever had an EEG, then the doctor was checking the electrical activity of the brain. The electrical signals in the body are another form of energy and without them we would be in serious trouble.

A very different example is the development of Kirlian photography in 1939. With this type of photography, we can literally see the outline of an electrical discharge around items such as a leaf, a fingertip, or a coin. Google "Kirlian" to see some cool photographs.

Our next example also involves photography. During the 1990s, a researcher from Japan named Masaru Emoto began doing experiments with water and high-speed photography to document his results. In 2001, he published a book called, "The Hidden Messages in Water", in order to share his research with a wider audience.

Emoto had developed an interest in studying water, and in his research he realized that water has the capability to copy and memorize information from its environment. He also discovered that when he froze a small sample of water it formed crystals which he could photograph. Putting these two insights together led to some fascinating discoveries.

Emoto started by taking samples of water from nature - spring water, lake water, polluted water - freezing the samples, taking pictures of the resulting crystals, and comparing the pictures. What he discovered surprised him. The less polluted the water sample, the more elegant and beautiful were the crystal formations.

Then his research assistant made an interesting suggestion. What if you exposed an unpolluted sample of water to different types of music? Emoto knew that the vibrations of music have an effect on water. Would different types of music result in different crystal formations? The answer was a resounding yes. They exposed identical samples of distilled water to classical music and consistently found "well-formed crystals with distinct characteristics. In contrast, the water exposed to violent heavy-metal music resulted in fragmented and malformed crystals at best." Fascinating.

Emoto and his researchers then wondered what would happen if they wrote different words on a piece of paper and wrapped the paper around tubes of identical water with the words facing in. Would the different energy of the different words result in different types of crystals being formed? The answer, again, was yes. "Water exposed to 'thank you' formed beautiful hexagonal crystals, but water exposed to the word 'fool' produced crystals similar to the water exposed to heavy-metal music, malformed and fragmented." Clearly, different words had a different vibration, a different energy signature, which was reflected in the water crystals. By the way, water exposed to the words "love and gratitude" had what Emoto considered to be the most beautiful crystal he had seen so far. He described it as if "the water had rejoiced and celebrated by creating a flower in bloom."

The research and photography of Emoto is all the more significant when you realize that water makes up to 60% of the human body. Clearly there is a distinctive energy in the different types of music and words. And this energy has a definite impact on the water in our bodies. This is a clear demonstration that there is unseen energy at work and that this energy contributes to how we feel when we listen to different types of music, when we are criticized and when we are praised.

You can check out YouTube for Masaru Emoto or Messages in Water to see examples of the different crystals.

The last example of how improved scientific instruments are allowing you to "see" energy is the development, in the 1960's, of the first Superconducting Quantum Interference Device (SQUID). The SQUID is a magnetometer which is capable of measuring the extremely subtle magnetic fields created by the human body. This is significant because magnetic fields are caused by the presence of an electric current and the SQUID is able to measure the tiny magnetic fields created by biochemical and physiological processes of the human body. In fact, the scientists have learned that the different tissues and organs in the body have their own unique magnetic fields, their own distinct energy signatures.

Today, with the accelerating development of computer technology, who knows what instruments we will develop that allow us to "see" that which cannot be directly seen? Suffice it to say that just as Galileo used an improved telescope to see the solar system, so are we now able to see the effects of an ever-present subtle energy system.

## Hard Evidence: Quantum physics

All of the above is suggestive, and perhaps persuasive, but is there any "hard" evidence to support the conclusion that energy is fundamental to reality? Evidence that is objective in nature? Indeed, there is. Physicists have realized the fundamental reality of energy and have been refining their understanding of it for over 100 years.

It is really easy to get off into the weeds when talking about quantum physics. However, we don't need to understand all of the main principles of quantum physics, or even the math, to grasp the key idea relevant to our discussion. Accordingly, I am going to skip over important concepts like complementarity, nonlocality and other such topics in order to focus on what is important to our well-being, understanding the fundamental reality of energy.

### The Very Large and the Very Small

During the 19th century, scientists began to observe a phenomenon that did not fit with the classical Newtonian paradigm of the world. Classical Newtonian physics breaks down when dealing with objects travelling very fast, have very strong gravity or are very small, such as atoms and what atoms are made of. The Newtonian paradigm was challenged in the 19th century in what is called the double-slit experiment which showed that light has both a particle and a wave characteristic to it. This did not fit with established physics which said that matter (and light) is made up of particle properties *or* wave properties, but not both at the same time.

At the beginning of the 20th century there was an increasing amount of experimental data that did not fit the existing Newtonian paradigm. Something was missing. Then, in 1901, a German physicist named Max Planck put forward the theory that items like radiation and light were made up of packets of energy with a fixed value, a notion that could not be reconciled with classical physics, especially when these packets of energy also showed wave properties.

You can think of Planck as being similar to Copernicus in Chapter 1.

They both had a deep respect for institutions and tradition, but their observations, logic and reason led them to question an accepted paradigm.

Into this historical setting stepped Albert Einstein, a man who was relatively unknown in scientific circles until 1905 when he published four critically important papers that provided a foundation for modern physics and changed the way we perceive time, space and matter.

For our purposes, we will focus on the fourth paper he published in 1905 on mass-energy equivalence. In it, he gave us the famous formula:

$$E=mc2$$

Translated, this means that anything having mass (matter) has a corresponding amount of energy. Further simplified, it means that everything we see as being physical, or made of matter/mass, is actually made up of energy. This is not what the paradigm of Descartes, dualism, Newton and classical physics said.

Going back to our example of Copernicus in Chapter 1, Einstein would be similar to Newton. The difference is that when Newton wrote in the 17th century, he was building on the ideas of Copernicus and the research of Galileo. Einstein, by comparison, skipped the accumulation of evidence stage before offering up his theory. Einstein would have gone down in history as an eccentric except that his thinking led to further experimentation which then confirmed his theories. Researchers had to shift the way they looked at the world and develop the appropriate scientific instruments/experiments in order to test Einstein's theory.

When the paradigm for the position of the earth/sun in our solar system was changed, it went Copernicus-Galileo-Newton, with the resulting development of classical Newtonian physics. When the paradigm for the role of energy in the 20th century was changed, it went Planck-Einstein and many scientists experimentally confirming Einstein's theories.

$E=mc2$. So how does this relate to self-help?

Since the realization that energy is fundamental to the material world, the question can be asked, is energy fundamental to the non-material world? The examples I gave at the beginning of this chapter would suggest that it is.

It is helpful to realize that energy can take many different forms, just like water. Water can be liquid, solid or vapor, but it is still water. Similarly, I would suggest that everything is a form of energy, we just experience energy in a multitude of ways.

What if there is an energy component to our emotions, beliefs, and memories? If that is true, then if we learn to shift the energy of an emotion, belief or memory, we can change the item itself. This expanded understanding would sound crazy until you realize this understanding was common across many cultures up until Descartes and the adoption of a dualistic paradigm.

Einstein focused on the material world and said Energy=mass. We are focusing on the nonmaterial world and saying that everything is a form of Energy.

At this place in our journey of understanding, I think it is important to point out that Einstein did not make Newton wrong. He added to Newton and pointed toward a larger picture of reality where all matter is made up of energy and operates according to Newton's principles at the day-to-day level of reality, while working according to quantum physics principles at the subatomic level of reality. Both are true. Newton's paradigm was simply incomplete.

In the same way, dualism, which we discussed in Chapter 2, is not wrong, it's simply incomplete.

Similarly, saying that nonmaterial items such as emotions, beliefs, and memories have an energy component to them does not deny the truths of contemporary psychology. Contemporary psychology, and by extension traditional self-help, are not wrong -- they are just an incomplete understanding of their subject matter. Just as mod- ern day physics use what is helpful from Newton while adding in what is helpful from quantum physics, so can we use what is helpful from contemporary psychology and self-help while adding in an expanded understanding of energy.

To quote Max Planck, a German physicist and considered the father of quantum physics:

"As a man who has devoted his whole life to the most clear-headed science, to the study of matter, I can tell you as a result of my research about the atoms this much: There is no matter as such! All matter originates and exists only by virtue of a force which brings the particles of an atom to vibration and holds this most minute solar system of the atom together We must assume behind this force the existence of a ***conscious and intelligent Mind*** (emphasis mine). This Mind is the matrix of all matter."

## Understanding the Human Condition: Current Research

Out of the scientific understandings that have emerged from the research of quantum physics in the last century, the fields of energy psychology and energy medicine have gained wider recognition over the last twenty years. The pace of research into these areas has accelerated as studies have been published and the stories of people who have been directly helped by these approaches has spread.

Authors such as David Feinstein. Ph.D., Bruce Lipton, Ph.D., William Tiller, Ph.D., Dawson Church, Amit Goswami, Ph.D., William Bengston, Ph.D., James Oschman, Ph.D., Donna Eden, and many others have made significant contributions to our understanding and the development of these fields. They are taking under standings of the human condition that have been recognized for centuries and bringing the rigor of scientific investigation to them in order to further validate their truth.

For those who would like to dive deeper into the current research I would bring two organizations to your attention.

The first is the HeartMath Institute. To quote from their website, "The HeartMath Institute (HMI) researches heart-brain communication and its relationship to managing stress, increasing coherence and deepening our connection to self and others. HMI's scientists also explore the electrophysiology of intuition and how all things are interconnected. Since 1991, the HeartMath Institute has researched and developed reliable, scientifically validated tools and technologies that help people improve their emotional balance, health and performance. HMI also has conducted intriguing research on how the heart's magnetic field radiates outside the body and can affect other people."

I have found their writings on heart-brain communication, the interconnection of all things and the coherent power of love to be especially helpful in developing an effective self-help approach.

The second organization is the Association for Comprehensive Energy Psychology (ACEP). This is the principal national organization for energy psychology, an organization in which I am a Certified Energy Health Practitioner.

If you go to their website, you will find over 100 published studies documenting the efficacy of various energy psychology techniques such as EFT, TAB, TAT and many others.

In sum, there is an ever-expanding base of research supporting what has been known for centuries, that everything is a form of energy and that we individually have an energy system. We just took a detour by embracing a dualistic paradigm of reality and becoming blind to the fundamental role of energy in our reality.

## A Brief History: Awareness of Energy Isn't New

It may seem odd that I am sharing evidence from history after talking about scientific research and highlighting other indicators pointing toward the existence of energy in everything, including a subtle energy system in each of us. The reason is that this understanding of energy and reality is not new. The understanding that there is an energetic web to life and that we need to learn how to care for our personal energy system is an understanding that has existed across multiple cultures and over thousands of years. Western culture abandoned the understanding of energy because it could not see, touch, or measure it. Now is our opportunity to benefit from renewing our understanding of what has always been known.

Our historical tour begins in the Indus Valley of northwest India and Pakistan in 3300 BC. Here we find the foundations of Ayurvedic medicine. Ayurveda means ayur (life) veda (knowledge or science) and was first recorded in the Veda texts approximately 1,200 years ago. Prior to that time, this knowledge had been passed down orally for over 1,000 years.

A central tenet of Ayurveda is that life is a combination of body, mind, senses, and spirit. Further, it teaches that nothing exists apart from a Supreme Intelligence/Consciousness - an elemental, all pervading, spirit-energy that expresses itself in and through creation. This spirit-energy, or life force, is called prana. Consistent with this fundamental understanding of life, Ayurvedic medicine focuses on maintaining the balance between mind, body, and spirit with the emphasis being on maintaining good health rather than curing illness.

So, we can see that the idea of an energy system being present in the human body, and its being an important part of health and well-being, has been around for approximately 5,000 years.

Next, let's go a bit north and east to China. Traditional Chinese Medicine (TCM) sees the cosmos (and individual people) as being made up of qi (chee) which is understood as including all forms of energy, from the material (such as the earth, your computer, and flesh and blood) to the most immaterial (light, heat, thought, and emotion). Similar to India and Ayurvedic medicine, a primary focus of TCM is the nurturing of life rather than the curing of illness. It is based on the basic principle that any system in harmony tends toward health and well-being.

Probably the most familiar TCM technique is the practice of acupuncture. Acupuncture uses specific points on the body in order to balance the flow of qi (energy) in the body.

I am noting the two cultures with the longest documented medical traditions, and their understanding of the fundamental importance of prana/qi/energy in their medical practices, but they are not alone. Concepts similar to prana and qi can be found in the cultures of the Igbo (modern day Nigeria), ancient Greece, traditional Hawaii, Tibet, Mayan, indigenous people of North America, Jewish culture, and the concept of vital energy in West- ern philosophy.

In short, the focus on dualism and the denial of energy as a fundamental part of creation and health, is a mere blip in the historical record. We are well served to use our current scientific understandings to rebalance our understanding of the importance of energy and to use this time-tested knowledge for our well-being today.

As Albert Szent-Györgyi, the 1937 Nobel Laureate in Medicine so aptly put it:

"The cell is a machine driven by energy. It can thus be approached by studying matter, or by studying energy. In every culture and in every medical tradition before ours, healing was accomplished by moving energy."

## We Can Shift Now

In wrapping up this chapter, it is clear that with the increasing sophistication of our scientific instruments we are renewing our understanding of and validating the ancient knowledge that everything is a form of energy and that we have a subtle energy system as part of our makeup.

It was by making this paradigm shift in how I saw myself that I was able to begin resolving personal challenges that had caused me pain for decades, regardless of the counseling I received or the self-help techniques I used. When I realized that maybe my problems were not mind/body problems, but rather were mind/body/energy problems with everything being a form of energy, I began to experience breakthroughs and realize greater peace and serenity in my life. I realized I had been using a 2D (mind/body) approach to solve 3D (mind/body/energy) problems. No wonder traditional self-help got me 2/3 of the way toward a solution and left me frustrated!

So now I was convinced that I have an energy system and everything is a form of energy. I had recovered what had been known by many cultures over thousands of years. What now? How did I make this understanding practical so that it helped me today and going forward?

How did I use this information and understanding to help me with my ODSR and anger issues?

Those questions lead us into the next chapter of the journey, a journey toward gaining new hope for our self-help.

# Resources

Eben Alexander, M.D., *Proof of Heaven: A Neurosurgeon's Journey into the Afterlife*, (New York: Simon & Schuster, 2012)

Masaru Emoto, *The Hidden Messages in Water*, (New York: Atria Books, 2005)

Jill Bolte Taylor, Ph.D., *My Stroke of Insight: A Brain Scientist's Personal Journey*, (Viking Penguin, 2008)

HeartMath Institute: www.heartmath.org

Association for Comprehensive Energy Psychology: www.energypsych. org

# Part 2

# My "Aha"

# Chapter 4

# A 2D Paradigm

*I*n the first part of this book we looked at the traditional approach to self-help and the assumptions behind the traditional approach. We also looked at some of the scientific discoveries and understandings over the last one hundred years which compel us to reexamine our assumptions and which provide a basis for an improved, more empowering approach to self-help.

In this section of the book, I will introduce you to three diagrams which will help to illustrate the concepts from the first section. I will provide you with a couple of graphic representations which make it easier to compare and contrast the dualistic (2D) and energy (3D) approaches to self-help. I will also share with you some of the insights that I have gleaned from the wide range of books I have read, trainings I have participated in and experiences I have received over the last 40+ years. These are key insights that have helped me to move through my ODSR and anger challenges, helped me in my journey toward greater serenity, have helped my clients and which can help you.

## Aha...

Being convinced that I have an energy system and that everything is a form of energy, and having experienced relief from various emotional hurts by using energy techniques like EFT and NLP, I continued to receive training in energy techniques. I gained an understanding of the basics on *why* these techniques worked, but it bothered me that I couldn't get a clear picture of *how* they worked. And it bothered me that I could not present a diagram of what was happening to make it easier for my students when I taught a class on how to use an energy technique to help yourself.

Then, one day in 2014, I was reading "Stress Management for Dummies" by Allen Elkin, Ph.D., and came across a description of the ABC model of stress from the work of the psychologist Dr. Albert Ellis.

$$A \rightarrow B \rightarrow C \text{ where}$$

A is the Activating event or potentially stressful situation

B is your Beliefs, thoughts, or perceptions about A

C is the emotional Consequence of stress that results from holding those beliefs

When I read this, an image flashed in my mind of how to diagram this process and, better yet, how to adapt the diagram to bring in the role of energy. My brothers, who are both engineers, would be impressed! More importantly, though, was that I now had a tool which provided a clear comparison between a mind/ body (2D) approach to emotional distress and a mind/body/energy (3D) approach.

In this chapter I will walk you through the 2D Perception Diagram. It represents the paradigm used by Dr. Ellis and by traditional self-help techniques. I will also offer some insights about the nature of events, emotions, beliefs, and memories that will assist you in moving through those items which have caused you distress.

# A 2D Paradigm

Sometimes the best way to explain something visual is to walk through each piece of it, describing the importance of each element. Take a look at the 2D Perception diagram below as I describe each of the components in the diagram.

## 2D PERCEPTION DIAGRAM

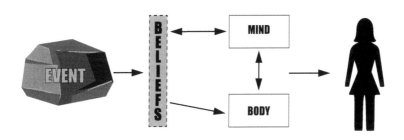

### Event

At the far left you will see a boulder with the word "Event" on it. An "Event" refers to anything that has happened, is happening or will happen in your life. Our lives are made up of a series of events or experiences which have no meaning in and of themselves.

This is a key point. Events have no inherent meaning, no meaning in and of themselves. All events in our lives are inherently neutral.

This can be a surprising realization since we typically assume that past events have an inherent meaning which we have always felt and heard running through our thoughts. So even though it may seem repetitive, I believe it is important to state this again, the events in our lives do not have any intrinsic meaning. Events are neutral.

We give any event its meaning depending on the beliefs through which we see them. What Albert Ellis said about an event producing stress is true about all events, and all the emotions that arise from those events in our lives. However, it's not what happened that matters, but how we perceive and remember what happened that makes a difference in how the event and the memory of the event impacts us in the short and long term.

**Now, we can either *react* or *respond* to the events in our lives.**

When an event elicits a strong emotion - "pushes our buttons" - we *react*. We find ourselves acting without thinking. An example of this would be road rage. However, when an event does not elicit a strong emotion in us, we can *respond*. When we respond, we are able to breathe first and think through how we want to act.

So why do some events cause us to react, while others do not? I would suggest that it depends on whether or not we perceive the event to be a threat to our physical or emotional safety.

It's easy to understand this concept when we think of our physical safety. As humans, we instinctively flee, fight, or freeze when our physical safety is threatened. If you're in the wild and a lion starts moving toward you, you are likely to react and move away, because it is a threat to your safety. But at the zoo, where the lion is behind a fence when it starts moving toward you, you are less likely to feel threatened and will probably respond by staying where you are.

This dynamic is the same with the emotional events in our lives. When we encounter an event where we feel our emotional safety is threatened, we react. When we feel emotionally safe, we are able to respond. For instance, some people feel supported and appreciated by their boss or supervisor, so when the boss walks over to their desk they do not react by becoming tense and guarded, they are able to respond to the event (the boss walking over to the desk). However, if you have experienced your supervisor as being overly critical, then you are likely to perceive them as a threat to your emotional safety and will react differently than if you felt safe with your supervisor. The feeling of not being emotionally safe results in a highly charged emotional state. This dynamic is true for any event, place, or person with which we have had a highly charged emotional experience. The more charged the emotional experience we associate with the occurrence of something in the present, the more likely we are to react rather than respond.

The event is the same. Your supervisor walking into the room is a neutral event – it has no meaning in and of itself. You give the event its meaning by the way in which you perceive it. This is true for all of us and for any event that occurs in our lives.

Let this sink in for a moment.

Your mind may be arguing with me right now. That reaction is completely normal. It is natural to think or feel that some events are not neutral, that they have an intrinsic negativity to them.

As I mentioned in the Introduction, I served in the Air Force at the end of the Vietnam War and for a few years afterward. As a veteran, and as a person who enjoys helping other people, I have a particular interest in PTSD (Post Traumatic Stress Disorder) and helping those who are suffering from PTSD. Isn't the event underlying the onset of PTSD inherently negative? That is a natural conclusion, however it is an inaccurate one. Why, for instance, can two people be exposed to the exact same event and one develops PTSD while the other does not? If the event were inherently negative, then everyone exposed to it would be impacted equally. In fact, the different reactions and responses to the event are largely determined by how the individual perceives, experiences, and processes the event. The event is given its meaning by the way it is perceived.

This is not to be critical of anyone who has a strong, debilitating reaction to an event in their life. We all have these reactions to one extent or another. The larger point that I am trying to emphasize here is that there is great hope and freedom in realizing that our ongoing negative reactions to a past event are not a life sentence. Our reaction to a past event is determined by how we perceived that event at the time and by the way we have continued to perceive it. It is liberating to realize we have the ability to shift how we perceive any past event and thus influence our ability to respond rather than react to its being part of our history.

We do not have to be permanently scarred by any past event and have our serenity or enjoyment of life permanently limited by what happened to us in the past. We can grow and heal into a place where we can acknowledge what happened to us, acknowledge that it was unwanted, know that we are physically and emotionally safe today and choose to change the way we perceive that past event. We can grow and heal into a place where we are able to respond, rather than react, to anything that reminds us of that past event in the present moment. By balancing the energy around any specific event, we can heal and shift our perception of what any extreme physical or emotional event means to us today. This may seem hard to believe in this moment, but in my personal experience and my professional experience of dealing with hundreds of clients, this is a profound truth. Understanding that an event is intrinsically neutral can provide us with a great deal of hope. It does not help us to believe that the meaning we give to an event is intrinsic to the event. To use a more lighthearted example, I could believe that the embarrassment I felt at a party in the 9th grade is intrinsic to all parties, and that going to any party runs the risk of feeling embarrassing. Thank goodness it's not true.

What happened is neutral. It only has the meaning you and I give to an event today that matters. And that meaning depends upon how you choose to see the event.

It is liberating and a source of hope when you realize that there is no intrinsic meaning to any event from your past. You have the power to change the way you see past events and thus change the meaning and their emotional impact on you.

It was freeing for me to realize that the past events I felt were a genesis for my anger and ODSR and had no intrinsic meaning. At the time that those events occurred in my life, I perceived them through the beliefs that I had acquired or learned up to that time. Now I understood I could choose to perceive those events differently and change the impact they would have on the quality of my life going forward.

## Beliefs

Looking again at the 2D diagram, you will see an arrow going from "Event" toward "Beliefs", which is in a dotted box.

The border is dotted for a purpose. Your beliefs form a filter through which you perceive, or see, an event. It is important to grasp the understanding that any belief you have operates as a filter and colors everything you see. For example, when you put-on rose-colored glasses the world appears differently than when you wear the yellow tinted glasses.

It is because of your beliefs that you give a particular meaning to an event - which is neutral in and of itself.

The other reason that "Beliefs" is in a dotted box is that all beliefs are optional. They are not cast in stone. All beliefs are learned, both consciously and unconsciously.

Let me repeat that statement because it is so important and potentially so liberating, all beliefs are learned.

Your beliefs were not determined at your time of birth. They are not fixed because of your family. We are not branded by our beliefs. Beliefs are learned.

Think about it. Have you ever changed your mind (belief) about a particular type of food, a musical group or a person?

The fact that you have the ability to change your belief about one thing, means that you can change your belief about anything. Consequently, you are free to choose how you see any event in your life. I agree it does not always feel like we are free to choose how we see an event, but the deeper and more profound truth is that we are free to choose.

Now, this understanding needs to be tempered by the fact that most of our beliefs are unconscious and were learned without us knowing it. So, let's show ourselves a little kindness as we grasp the reality that *all of us* have picked up beliefs during our lifetime which we did not intentionally choose, but which color how we see the events around us nonetheless. Let's grab hold of the freedom and power this realization gives us to learn how to change those beliefs which no longer serve us into beliefs that empower us.

Even though we unknowingly learned a belief in the past, we can change that learning if we so desire. You can take on a new belief, just like you did about that food you didn't like as a kid, but now enjoy. We can identify beliefs which have not served us well, or which served us in the past but are no longer serving us, and take on a new belief or learning. (More on how to do this later in the book.) We have the freedom to take on new beliefs so that we perceive events in a different way and then are able to respond rather than react to any given event.

So, if beliefs are learned, where did we learn them? The beliefs we carry around with us are learned from a variety of sources. Let me offer up three of those sources here.

First, we learn beliefs from our caretakers and those we consider to be authority figures. Prior to the age of 7 (approximately), we take on beliefs with no conscious thought involved. These are called implicit beliefs. It's more like we "pick up" beliefs, rather than learn them. We depend on our caretakers to keep us physically and emotionally safe. In addition, the critical reasoning capacity of the brain is not yet developed so we don't have the capacity to critique the beliefs which are being modeled for us. As a result, we see the world the same way they do, unknowingly, in order to feel that we belong and will be protected.

The same goes for authority figures, though not quite as acutely as with those whom we depend on for our safety. We all learned beliefs from our teachers and other significant people in our lives. We trusted and accepted these people in our lives, we wanted to belong to the tribe they represented, so we accepted the way that they saw the world.

Second, we learn beliefs from significant emotional experiences. When something happens in your life that was emotionally charged for you, you take on an understanding from it. You take on a "rule of life". You may not consciously know what you are learning, but you do take on beliefs that color how you will see similar events in the future. For example, if you had a scary experience with an animal at some point in your life, then you could start to associate fear with that animal, and take on a belief that this particular animal cannot be trusted and should be avoided.

Remember the example in the first chapter, of my dad jumping out of his shoes when he touched the skin of a rattlesnake that I had in my bedroom? Something had happened earlier in his life that gave him a fear of snakes. He didn't learn it from a book. I don't know if my dad even knew why he reacted to snakes the way that he did. He just knew that he did, and avoided them. There was some significant emotional experience earlier in his life which created an unconscious, implicit belief that he should react to snakes with fear.

A third way that we learn beliefs is from the reference groups that we have. Reference groups are those people that you compare yourself to, and who you want to be accepted by. Examples of reference groups would be your family, friends, and community. The beliefs coming from these associations are explicit. That is, you are conscious that you hold certain beliefs. In an effort to fit into your environment, in order to have a sense of belonging and to feel safe, you took on the beliefs of a particular group.

My grandfather was a sharecropper in Tennessee during the 1930's. As a child, I spent many hours with him camping and fishing. I can recall specific instances when he was teaching me to have the same racial prejudices that he had, and I went along with him. He was my grandfather, and I trusted him, and I didn't know any better. But it so happens that I grew up in the San Francisco area of California, not as a sharecropper in Tennessee. As I made friends in school, I quickly learned that not everyone had the same beliefs about race. Fortunately, I was able to realize what I had been taught as a child and to decide that I did not want to keep the prejudicial beliefs of my grandfather. I chose to take on different beliefs. I am grateful for many things that he did teach me. I just decided we would have to disagree on certain beliefs . . . and I made sure I did not bring up the topic of racial prejudice around my grandfather.

So, our beliefs are both conscious and unconscious, both explicit and implicit, both learned and acquired. There are some beliefs you know you have and you can articulate them. You can say, "I believe this." And I can say, "Well, I believe that." And we could have a discussion about different beliefs.

Then there are other beliefs that are unconscious. These are beliefs which have been imprinted on us, and then reinforced over our lifetime. We typically are not aware of these beliefs until we find ourselves reacting to something or someone and don't know why we are reacting in such a manner. You can probably think of times when you did this with a boyfriend, girlfriend, or a loved one.

I am not sure what the ratio of conscious and unconscious beliefs are for the typical person, but the research is clear that the vast majority of our beliefs are unconscious.

It's an interesting tendency of human beings that once we have taken on a belief, we then filter the information that we take in, in order to confirm that belief. We see what we are looking for. This is just the way our brains work. Because there is so much data and stimulus around us at any given time, we need to filter out a lot of it in order to stay sane. This results in our unconsciously reinforcing beliefs which were likely unconsciously acquired. So, we have our beliefs, our rules of life and we filter all incoming information accordingly. It is not instinctive to question our beliefs, we couldn't survive if we were constantly reviewing each rule of life, each belief that we held.

Whether beliefs are conscious or unconscious, the important point is that they are all learned. They are not cast in stone. They are not predetermined. They are not genetic. They are learned. This makes all of our beliefs optional. If a belief you picked up along the way is not serving what is highest and best for you now, then you have the option to choose a belief that will be more empowering for you . . . a belief that brings you greater peace and serenity.

Beliefs are initially taken on in order to keep us feeling safe, both physically and emotionally. They kept us part of a family, part of a group. They kept us safe from threats we perceived to be around us. Now that we are older, we can find ways to feel and be safe, while changing those beliefs that no longer serve us. Rest assured, the Pondera Process® I will share with you later in the book will make it much easier to identify and shift those beliefs which no longer serve you, while continuing to feel safe.

The important point right now is to understand that no belief, be it conscious or unconscious, is something you have to be stuck with. None of your beliefs have to be permanent. None of them are genetically determined. We are not branded by our beliefs. This was an incredibly liberating understanding for me and can be a source of hope and inspiration for you as well.

Again, the beliefs we hold are just a filter through which we see events. If you have an old, limiting belief which is causing you pain, then you can trade it in for a new, empowering belief whenever you are ready. That may sound outrageous and over-the-top to you, but

I assure you it is true. When you approach the changing of a belief from a 2D paradigm it can be very difficult, but when you approach the changing of a belief from a 3D paradigm it becomes much easier. If you are willing and hold an intention to let go of limiting beliefs, then the Pondera Process® can make that shift simple and quite doable.

## Mind

Going back to the 2D Perception Diagram, the next area to discuss is the "Mind". The first item to clarify is making a distinction between "mind" and "brain". In contemporary usage the two items are often used interchangeably or mixed together. The mind is generally associated with qualities such as consciousness, perception, thinking, judgement, feeling, and memory. In contrast, the brain is generally considered to be a physical organ like your heart or liver. The brain is a physical object that can be seen while the mind is not. For those who take a hard scientific view of life, the brain is considered to be a computer running the machine that is your body and the mind is a product of the brain's physical process.

How you see the mind and the brain depends on the assumptions and beliefs you bring to the subject. The more materialistic you are (seeing everything as being matter or a byproduct of the interactions of matter) the more emphasis you put on the mind as being a byproduct of the brain.

It is clear that the brain does work like a computer, receiving/processing inputs and generating outputs. Depending on how we perceive an event, which depends on the belief we are filtering our perception through, we take that input into our brain. At that point a whole series of actions start to occur automatically – not the least of which is that the brain triggers a release of chemical in forms such as peptides and hormones into the bloodstream. These chemicals in turn affect the activity of our glands, organs, muscles, and other body parts.

But this understanding of the brain as a computer does not mean that the mind has to be an output of its operation. The mind is much greater than our brain. In Buddhist teachings, the body (including the brain) is compared to a guest house and the mind is a guest dwelling within it.

While Descartes and the original understanding of dualism saw the mind in loftier terms, as having a transcendent quality to it, contemporary medicine (2D medicine) has chosen to see the mind as being a byproduct of the brain.

Just as we can look at the cell as a machine or as an energy process, the answer to the mind or brain question is more of a both/and answer rather than an either/or option. I think this mind/brain tension can be partially resolved when we look at the 3D Perception Diagram and introduce the role of energy into this dynamic interaction.

All of this can muddy what is meant by "mind". Regardless of how you look at the mind/brain relationship, they have been joined together as "mind" in contemporary medicine and in traditional self-help writings. For our purposes, we can put both the mind and brain into the "mind" box and think of the brain as being the hardware in a computer, the mind as being the programs or applications we choose, and beliefs as being the operating system with which the mind is compatible.

In the diagram, you also see an arrow pointing in both directions from "Beliefs" to "Mind" and from "Mind" to "Body". That's because there is a dynamic interplay between these three elements. This interplay can be demonstrated by the placebo effect and by psychosomatic illnesses.

Contemporary medicine knows that belief has an important role in the effectiveness of medications. Research suggests that as much as one third of the effect a medication has on an individual is due to the placebo effect, the positive effect received by an individual is due to the pre-existing belief that the medication will help. In contrast to the placebo effect is the reality of psychosomatic illnesses. You have heard the expression, "they worried themselves sick"? This statement can be literally true. When we worry to excess, it impairs our immune system and we are much more likely to become ill. There are many examples of people who have symptoms with no discernible biological reason for them and, in some cases, the symptoms disappear when their perception on life changes. It is your belief and how you perceive an event that triggers the mind/brain to release the chemicals that affect your body.

In addition, the arrow between "Mind" and "Beliefs" is pointing in both directions because in a dualistic, or 2D paradigm, it is maintained that the only way to change a belief is through your mind. The body is considered to be a machine and doesn't have the capacity to change a belief on its own.

As you will see in the next chapter, this is a limiting assumption of the 2D view on life and significantly contributes to the frustration with traditional self-help techniques.

This takes us to the last part of the 2D Perception Diagram, the "Body".

**Body**

Okay, to explain this piece of the diagram, I'm going to dip into my high school biology class. Stay with me, biology and chemistry were not my strengths so you know I will keep this pretty simple. We can look at the HPT axis, which stands for the hypothalamic-pituitary-thyroid axis, and its connection to the experience of stress as an illustration of the interplay between mind and body. The HPT is part of the neuroendocrine system which is responsible for regulating the body's' metabolism. It is also a central biological process in our experience of the physical sensations related to stress.

When the hypothalamus senses that the levels of thyroid hormones T3 and T4 in the body are low, it releases a hormone called TRH which stimulates the pituitary gland to produce TSH, which in turn stimulates the thyroid to produce thyroid hormone until levels in your bloodstream return to normal. The hypothalamus and the pituitary gland are located in the brain while the thyroid is in the neck area, just below the Adam's apple.

The HPT axis is a perfect example of how the mind and body work together automatically for the benefit of survival. It keeps the body's metabolism operating smoothly.

But the mind can also create illness when there is no outside cause for the problem. Take the example, once again, of psychosomatic illness. Have you ever known someone who became ill from too much worry or anger? Or whose chronic depression led to physical problems? There was no organic reason for the physical ailments, but the physical problems were no less real.

As we can see, the mind does have a powerful influence over the body, for both good and ill.

## Addicted to Emotions

Another important aspect to this discussion is the realization that people can become addicted to an emotion, whether that emotion be stress, anger, worry or any other particular emotion. For a variety of emotional and physical reasons, it is not uncommon for people to become dependent on feeling a particular emotion. People have reported physical withdrawal symptoms when they don't get their "emotional fix". Walk through any high school or college campus, and you will see students who wear stress as a badge of honor. Not to mention there are so many workplaces where if you don't look sufficiently stressed, it is assumed you are not working hard enough. For so many, the notion that you could be a student or productive worker without being stressed out "just doesn't feel right".

Perhaps a clearer example of how we can become addicted to an emotional state is to look at adrenaline junkies. Those are people who love the thrill of physical or emotional danger and how it makes them feel. Loving the adrenaline rush in your body is fine, unless it leads you to compromise other areas of your life. Think of the gambler who loves the thrill of the horse races – which is fine until they gamble away the rent money.

Or, how about anger? I have worked with clients who were addicted to anger. Being angry was an emotional defense for them and it made them feel physically powerful. But when you tap into anger on a regular basis, your body becomes accustomed to how that feels and then it feels uncomfortable when you are not angry. So, consciously or unconsciously, you look for something to be angry about.

I know this particular pattern well. I was my own first client in learning how to let go of anger.

Addiction to an emotion can happen with many emotions, not just stress, adrenaline, or anger. I have encountered people who are addicted to fear, guilt, shame, worry, and other emotions. All of these produced a benefit to them at one time, but they then became dependent on that emotion. They did not like the feeling of being without a familiar emotion so they lived life in a way that would create the emotion they craved.

All of the above are examples of how beliefs and perception affect us biologically. However, I encourage you to remember that our DNA and how our body works is not deterministic. We are not trapped by our DNA. Instead, we can use our free will to impact what happens in our brain and body by changing the beliefs we use to filter life through, by changing the way we perceive events in our life.

Now, most of our conventional medicine and teaching in the self-help industry stops right here. They choose to perceive the challenges of life through a two-dimensional mind/body, or 2D, paradigm.

But what if life and its challenges are really a 3D experience? That was the question I began to ask myself as I learned more and more about the vital role energy plays in our life. So, when I went back and looked at the work of Dr. Albert Ellis, it occurred to me that stress, and by extension everything else, could be seen through a 3D paradigm – a paradigm that sees life as a mind/body/energy experience. This led me to expand the 2D Perception Diagram and to develop the 3D Perception Diagram described in the next chapter.

# Resources

Allen Elkin, Ph.D., *Stress Management for Dummies* (New York: Wiley Publishing, 1999)

# Chapter 5

# A 3D Paradigm

*L*et's now take a look at the 3D Perception Diagram and see how it complements and expands on the 2D Perception Diagram.

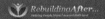

## 3D PERCEPTION DIAGRAM

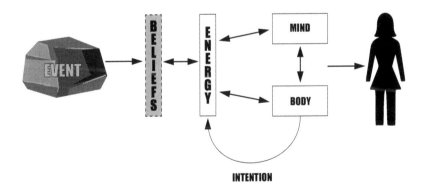

The previous diagram illustrates the traditional mind/body allopathic approach toward well-being. But what if we know that each person has a subtle energy system? What does that look like?

Let's start by recalling the quote from Albert Szent-Györgyi:

> "The cell is a machine driven by energy. It can thus be approached by studying matter or by studying energy. In every culture and in every medical tradition before ours, healing was accomplished by moving energy."

The 2D paradigm is not wrong, it is incomplete. The 2D paradigm sees the cell, and nature in general, as a machine. While there is truth in that perception, it is only part of the picture. It's as if you were putting together a jigsaw puzzle and as you place the last piece you have left in the box, you realize that there is a piece missing. You would still have pieced together a picture with your puzzle, but the picture would be incomplete.

It is helpful to know that throughout history many different cultures have accepted and viewed energy as a fundamental part of life. The adoption of dualism and the resultant denial of energy as a part of life is unique to our time. While there have been benefits from adopting a 2D paradigm, there have also been significant drawbacks. Living life from a 2D perspective is like trying to live life with one hand tied behind your back. You can do it, but life is much easier when you use both hands. Wouldn't it be better to keep the benefits of a 2D approach to life, add an understanding of energy to it, and enjoy the benefits of working with a complete picture of life?

I and many of my clients have benefited from expanding our paradigm, our understanding of how we operate, to include our subtle energy system. By doing this we can intentionally use energy as a vital component of our well-being, the same way we care for our biological systems.

Looking at the 3D Perception Diagram, at first glance it looks like there are boxes and arrows going every which way. Don't despair. It really is simpler to understand than it may appear. It's just that we humans have a very dynamic, interrelated, mind/body/ energy system, and the more dynamic a system is, the more boxes and arrows there are!

## Event and Beliefs

You will notice that these two pieces of the 3D Perception diagram are the same as the 2D Perception Diagram. The change is in how we understand the way we process the events in our life which we are filtering through a particular belief.

## Energy

To understand what is really happening we need to remember what quantum physics has shown - everything is a form of energy. All the cells in our mind/body are made up of atoms which are energy at their core.

Accordingly, the obvious difference between the 2D and 3D Perception Diagrams is now we are including "Energy" into the process that guides what we think, feel, and do. But before we learn about how energy interacts with the mind and body, let's take a moment to talk about the human being's subtle energy system itself. I have repeatedly said we have such a system and pointed out how personal experiences, science, and history support its existence, but what is it?

Here are 10 fundamental concepts which will further contribute to your Energy Intelligence (EnQ) and help you to understand the rest of this book. Energy Intelligence (EnQ) is an adaptation of Emotional Intelligence (EQ), which is a helpful paradigm for understanding and managing emotions. I describe EnQ as "the ability to understand your body's energy system, to identify disruptions in your energy system and to restore balance, harmony, and flow to your energy system". Here are those 10 fundamental concepts:

1. Energy is a vital, dynamic force which flows into, through and from us.

2. A healthy energy system has a balanced and harmonious flow of energy continually circulating through it, the same way blood circulates through your body.

3. Our energy system is made up of meridians, which are similar to arteries and veins in that they carry energy to all parts of the body; chakras, we have seven centers or vortexes of spinning energy which are located along the midline of our bodies from the tailbone to the top of the head; and an aura, which is typically described as an egg-shaped ball of electromagnetic energy that surrounds the body. There are additional energy structures in the body, but these are the three primary ones.

4. Each aspect of our energy system is designed to move in a specific pattern which is unique to it and in harmony with the other energies.

5. Emotional and physical problems result when the normal flow, harmony, and balance of energy becomes blocked, stagnant, or scattered.

6. Disruption to the body's energy system can result from any type of significant physical or emotional experience.

7. Emotions, beliefs, and memories which create ongoing distress for you, and/or limit your experience of serenity, typically have a disrupted energy pattern associated with them.

8. Normal and healthy energy patterns can be restored through:
   - Tapping, holding, or massaging specific energy points on the body

- Tracing the hand along specific energy pathways
- Engaging in specific exercises or postures, such as in yoga
- Through intention and focused use of the mind
- And many more techniques

9. When a normal and healthy energy pattern is restored, the individual typically experiences a sense of relief, freedom, clarity, and serenity.

10. By intentionally shifting the energies around a distressing emotion, belief, or memory we can bring balance to whatever triggered the original distress and enable an individual to take on an emotion, belief, or interpretation of an event (memory) that serves what is highest and best for them.

Having the above concepts as a foundation, let's briefly review how your energy system interacts with your beliefs, body, and mind.

## Energy ⟷ Beliefs

When you perceive an event through the belief or filter of your choosing, it is your energy system that is impacted first and then triggers responses from the mind/body. It's natural to think that our perception of an event comes through our eyes into the mind and then affects the body. While this is true, your energy system is actually picking up the energy you give the event before it ever registers in your mind. That, in turn, is what is triggering the mind/body response. Energy travels much faster than any mental or biological process. It's wild, but true!

Going back to the 3D Perception Diagram, you also see an arrow which connects back to the "Beliefs" box. Remember our basic premise, which is everything is a form of energy - including our beliefs. Recall the example of how an audience's thoughts impacted the muscle strength of the volunteer. I also know that beliefs are a form of energy because I have helped hundreds of people to use their energy system to shift from a belief that caused them distress, to a belief that empowered them. When you learn how to shift the energy of a belief, you can shift or change the belief itself. Hence, the arrow is pointed on both ends to show that information is flowing in both directions and that you can change a belief by changing the energy around it.

## Energy ⟷ Mind

As with the body, tons of books have been written about the relationship between the mind and energy. Do a simple search on "meditation" and you'll see what I mean. And just like the body, we can study the mind as matter or as energy.

The idea that I want to emphasize here is that all emotions, beliefs, and memories are a form of energy and have a unique energy signature - just like different foods. If you don't have a background in energy psychology, then this is a very different way of looking at a familiar topic.

There are two ways to change an emotion, belief, or memory. One way is to treat it as matter (loosely speaking) and do it with your mind and willpower. The other way is to treat them as a form of energy and to shift the energy through intention. Both ways will work. Shifting the energy is easier and more effective - because the emotion, belief, or memory is a form of energy to begin with.

Consider an example such as reducing the level of stress in your life. You can use any number of traditional self-help techniques such as controlling your breathing, focusing your mind on a calming thought or image, using affirmations and many other techniques, all requiring you to consciously use your will to change your emotional state. Or you can use an energy psychology technique such as the Pondera Process®, to use your intention and balance out the disrupted energy you are feeling. Both work, but the energy approach works better.

So, the arrow points in both directions between the mind and energy because there is a dynamic interplay between the two and a change in either one of them impacts the other.

## Energy ↔ Body

Lots and lots of books have been written on the relationship between energy and the body. A quick check of Amazon shows that there are over 10,000 books on "body energy".

However, I am going to keep it basic by noting that your energy system provides an infrastructure for your physical body, similar to the way your bones do. When there is a disruption in the normal flow of your energy system you will feel it in your body. For example, when you feel nervous or anxious, you are feeling the physical manifestation of the scattering of your energy. When you feel a discomfort in the pit of your stomach, you are feeling your energy being blocked.

It is easy to feel the energy in your body once you know that it exists. It is the source of that familiar feeling of distress in your stomach, neck, shoulders, and other areas of your body. When we go through the Pondera Process®, one of the steps is to see where you feel the emotion, belief, or memory in your body. When I ask my clients this question, they can clearly feel their disrupted energy in their body over 90% of the time.

There is an entire discipline called Energy Medicine dedicated to helping the body heal through caring for the energy system. If you would like more information on this dynamic relationship, I would recommend exploring the work of Donna Eden. I have provided a link to her website in the resources section of this chapter.

Just as the health of your energy system impacts your body, you also can impact your energy system through your body. You can impact your energy system through what you eat and by what you do. For example, when you eat foods that are natural and don't have a bunch of preservatives you will feel better. The reason you feel better is that food is another form of energy, has an energy signature just like anything else, and has an impact on your energy system. When you eat foods that are closer to nature, they typically have a higher vibration to their energy signature which means that they will better support your energy system. Just as we can study the cell as matter or energy, so we can understand the impact of food on us as biology (matter) or energy.

Similarly, you can impact your energy system through movements such as yoga to improve the harmony, balance, and flow of energy in your body.

## Mind ↔ Body

The dynamic here is the same as in the 2D Perception Diagram. Just because we are introducing energy into our paradigm doesn't mean that the mind/body relationship changes. The difference is we now see the mind/body relationship as an expression or form of energy and realize that it is an open system which allows the input of energy, not a closed system as represented in the 2D paradigm. The mind and body continue to interact, with both being affected by any change in the energy which underlies both of them.

## Intention

In the Introduction, I described the Pondera Process® as combining scientific understandings, psychological insights, and spiritual truths. We then looked at the traditional 2D paradigm for understanding how our world operates. We also noted some of the scientific understandings over the last century which support the need for us to expand our understanding toward a 3D paradigm, as well as the need for us to reevaluate the assumptions of traditional self-help. In this section of the book, we are putting these scientific understandings into diagrams that make them a bit more understandable and much more practical. We are also introducing some psychological insights about the nature of events, emotions, beliefs, and memories that flow from using a 3D paradigm to view them. Now, with the inclusion of "intention" into the 3D Perception Diagram, I am introducing the first of several spiritual truths. Through intention, we are able to tap into a Source of energy greater than ourselves, begin to work with our personal energy system and bring a new power to self-help.

Common definitions of intention suggest that it means to have a strong purpose or aim to achieve a desired result. It typically has a psychological or personal-growth emphasis. However, this is a 2D definition and reflects an emphasis on willpower which comes from the self. A 3D definition of intention would be the conscious choice and purposeful connecting with the Source of all energy. So, for our purposes in the 3D paradigm, intention is the conscious choice to receive and allow an eternal and universal energy of Love into our personal energy system. A 2D definition of intention is marked by an emphasis on self, ego, power, striving, and control. In contrast, a 3D understanding of intention is marked by receiving, allowing, releasing, and participation. As you can see, instead of willpower and self, a 3D understanding of intention comes from free will and spirit/energy.

**Pure Love**

Let's take a few moments to unpack this expanded understanding of intention.

In Chapter 3 of this book, I endeavored to establish the understanding that everything is a form of energy. But where does this energy come from? Where does it originate?

I have read explanations for the origin of energy that run from the idea that it is a "field of energy" that just is, with no particular origin, to the understanding that we live in a conscious universe, to it comes from a particular Deity and carries a lot of religious overtones.

I doubt there is an objective, concrete answer to the question and there will always be an element of personal belief in any answer. That being said, let me share with you what I and my clients have found to be a working understanding. I come to this understanding having graduated from a Christian liberal arts college, having read a lot of books in the areas of science/philosophy/theology, and having over 10 years of experience in seeing what has consistently worked for myself and my clients. This is the evolved understanding that I ascribe to and which is assumed in the 3D paradigm.

I live and work from the premise that at the core of everything is an energy of pure Love. That we can connect with the energy of pure Love, a Love that is unconditional and desires what is highest and best for us, any time we choose to do so. This is a spiritual truth that has existed for millennia and across numerous cultures. It continues to be validated today by people who have had near death experiences and by people who have experienced an improvement in their emotional or physical well-being after intentionally connecting with the energy of pure Love.

I have found that this spiritual reality is not the domain of any one religion or faith, but rather it is a Love available to everyone. When I work with a client on something which is causing distress in their life, I ask them to tell me what they call that Presence which is greater than themselves, what they call that Presence which they feel when they are one with nature. Clients have used terms such as Source, Universe, Higher Power, God, Father, Mother Nature, and more. The positive results which they experienced were the same regardless of how they referred to the universal energy of pure Love.

Where does this energy of Love come from? Where does it originate? I don't know. It is the "I AM" of the Judeo-Christian tradition, the Brahma of the Hindu tradition, it is an understanding which is echoed in the other major religions. Regardless of origins, the energy of pure Love is present and available to all of us.

The consistent spiritual teaching, expressed in different ways by different people at different times, is that the energy of Love pre-exists anything created. That all things are ultimately an expression of this energy. It is an energy which vibrates so fast that we are unable to measure it with our 2D scientific instruments, we can only feel it. We can experience the positive results of its presence when we choose to tap into it through intention. It is a Presence that can be sensed and felt through an increased sensitivity to our own personal energy systems. Regardless of origin, the energy of pure Love is an all-pervasive, universal force that is present and available to all of us at any time.

Let me illustrate this dynamic by recounting the story of Mrs. Jonathan Edwards as described by William James, a noted American psychologist and philosopher, in his book *The Varieties of Religious Experience.*

"Last night was the sweetest night I ever had in my life. I never before, for so long a time together, enjoyed so much of the light and rest and sweetness of heaven in my soul, but without the least agitation of body during the whole time. Part of the night I lay awake, sometimes asleep, and sometimes between sleeping and waking. But all night I continued in a constant, clear, and lively sense of the heavenly sweetness of Christ's excellent love, of his nearness to me, and of my dearness to him; with an inexpressibly sweet calmness of soul in an entire rest in him. I seemed to myself to perceive a glow of divine love come down from the heart of Christ in heaven into my heart in a constant stream, like a stream or pencil of sweet light.

At the same time, my heart and soul all flowed out in love to Christ, so that there seemed to be a constant flowing and reflowing of heavenly love, and I appeared to myself to float or swim, in these bright, sweet beams, like the motes swimming in the beams of the sun, or the streams of his light which come in at the window. I think that what I felt each minute was worth more than all the outward comfort and pleasure which I had enjoyed in my whole life put together. It was pleasure, without the least sting, or any interruption. It was a sweetness, which my soul was lost in; it seemed to be all that my feeble frame could sustain... As I awoke early the next morning, it seemed to me that I had entirely done with myself. I felt that the opinions of the world concerning me were nothing, and that I had no more to do with any outward interest of my own than with that of a person whom I never saw. The glory of God seemed to swallow up every wish and desire of my heart."

In reading the above account of Mrs. Edwards' experience, I would encourage you not to be distracted by the language she uses to describe her experience. Her use of Christian symbols to express herself is because these are the words and concepts familiar to her time and place for describing an experience that is many ways beyond words.

What is important in the above account is to see the similarities, the spiritual truths, she is articulating and which are consistent in the spiritual writings of many cultures. The references to light, rest, sweetness, calmness of soul, comfort and pleasure, the flowing and reflowing of love, all of these are hallmarks of people who have allowed themselves to connect with the Love that is fundamental to our existence.

One spiritual truth I would highlight from Mrs. Edwards' account is her description of what "seemed to be a constant flowing and reflowing of heavenly love". This dynamic reciprocity of Love, the experience of receiving and giving of Love form an eternal Source, is possible through the free will exercise of intention. Mrs. Edwards would not have had this experience if she was not willing to first receive it and to then give it back in gratitude. In the end, the natural progression for anyone who allows themself to experience this reciprocity of Love is to realize and accept one's identity as being one with this Source of pure Love.

## Why does it Work?

OK, so why does allowing the energy of pure Love into our energy system make a difference to our well-being? As with the questions above about the origin of this energy, there have been many answers put forward. Let me give you two answers which can help to shed some light on what is happening.

First is the more scientific answer. One researcher who has done extensive work in this area is David R. Hawkins, M.D., Ph.D., whose seminal book on the subject is called *Power vs. Force*. In his research, Dr. Hawkins noted that different emotions had different energy frequencies, different vibrations, and that they each had a different impact on the body's muscle strength. Furthermore, he was able to use kinesiology to calibrate where a specific emotion fell on a scale of low to high frequency. His findings consistently showed that Love tested at the highest frequency of all emotions. This is significant because it indicates that Love is a higher frequency than any emotion that can cause you distress, Love is stronger and more powerful than any other emotion. I suspect that as scientific instruments become increasingly sophisticated, we will be able to more precisely measure the different emotions and their impact on our physiology.

My second answer is a working hypothesis that fits with the results I have seen. As a believer in pragmatic spirituality, I appreciate the research but I have a greater appreciation for the practical results myself and others receive from being open to allowing a Divine energy to support us. If we accept that limiting emotions, beliefs, and memories are forms of energy and have an energy sig nature, then by allowing the high vibration energy of pure, unconditional Love to enter our personal energy system we are able to free up blocked energy, balance scattered energy, and change the energy signature of a limiting emotion, belief, or memory. By allowing the higher vibration energy of pure Love to enter our energy system, we are able to shift and raise the vibration or frequency of what we are focusing on and thus increase the balance, harmony, and flow of energy within ourselves. This improvement in our energy system in turn allows us to access more empowering emotions and beliefs, and to reinterpret old memories in ways that better serve us now.

## Free Will and Personal Growth

Looking again at the 3D Perception Diagram you will see an arrow going from "Mind" to "Energy" with the word "Intention" below it. This arrow is to show that you have the ability to intentionally choose to allow Love to touch your energy system, which can then shift emotions, beliefs, and memories that cause you distress (more on this in the next chapter).

As I mentioned earlier in this discussion of "Intention", there is a difference between the traditional 2D definition of intention and the 3D definition of intention that I am using. The traditional understanding of intention is having a strong purpose or aim to achieve a desired result. This is an understanding which assumes a reliance upon self and places an emphasis on power, striving, and control. By contrast, a 3D understanding of intention assumes a reliance on Source and places an emphasis on allowing, releasing, and participation.

Intention is the exercise of your free will to make a conscious choice and purposeful connection with the Source of all energy, with pure Love, and allowing it to touch your energy system.

You and I have a choice, we can choose to connect with Source or we can choose to operate apart from Source. The problem has been that we were taught a 2D understanding of intention and have been making an unconscious choice to live a life separate from Source. We have been taught to approach self-help with an emphasis on disciplining the self. Now, by contrast, you are becoming aware and conscious of a larger reality. When you choose to approach life and self-help from a 3D understanding of reality, you are able to make a conscious choice to exercise your free will and to make a purposeful connection with Source.

The necessity for you and I to exercise free will in connecting with Source is an essential element to our personal growth. We are not required to have a 3D understanding of reality, we are free to live within the limitations of a 2D paradigm. We are free to rely on ourselves, rather than Source, if we so choose. However, the larger picture for personal growth and happiness is learning that we are 3D creations and learning how to make a purposeful connection with Source, learning how to participate with and be in alignment with Source in as many aspects of our lives as we can. It is from being in ever increasing alignment with Source that we experience true peace, serenity, and joy.

Since most of us live in a culture which is dominated by a 2D understanding of reality, and since most of us have been taught a 2D approach to self-help, it requires a conscious choice to approach life and our well-being from a 3D understanding.

Also, the very concept of growth implies the necessity of making a choice. While there are a few aspects of life, such as physical maturation, that occur without our making a choice, most growth in the various aspects of life do require a choice, be it conscious or unconscious. For example, the quality of our health is the result of the choices we make about food, exercise, etc. Similarly, the quality of our emotional life is the result of how we choose to address the stress, anger, guilt, fear, shame, etc. that are a part of everyone's life.

The flip side of growth requiring us to make choices is to take on a victim mentality. We are free to believe that we are destined by our DNA to have a particular quality of life, we are free to believe that our long-term happiness is determined by the quality of the parenting we experienced, and we are free to believe that well-being has been permanently scarred by a past experience. We are free to choose to be a victim because we are also free to choose not to be a victim.

My observation has been that many people fall into the victim trap for one of two reasons. Either they don't know that they have a choice, they don't know how to access a more empowering solution to their challenge; or two, they are receiving some ongoing benefits from being a victim. At some point in their life, they took on the identity of being a victim in order to cope emotionally with circumstances that felt overwhelming. They have not learned another way to cope with what happened to them apart from defining themselves as a victim.

The point is, growth requires the exercise of our free will to make a choice to grow through any particular challenge life brings our way. We are free to choose between tapping into the energy of Source, which is animated by love for us, and separating ourselves from Source. When we separate ourselves from Source, we end up relying on willpower and striving for serenity. We end up trying to control life in order to make ourselves feel happy. We end up striving for serenity rather than allowing serenity.

The larger truth is that serenity is something we receive, not something we achieve. It is the result of intentionally tapping into Source and allowing the energy of Love to flow into and through our life. When we choose a 3D approach to life's challenges, we can be in alignment with Source and an increased sense of serenity is the natural byproduct.

As you can see, our capacity for free will is a necessary component of personal growth. When you adhere to a 2D view of life you put your focus on yourself and cut yourself off from this ever present, universal Source of loving energy.

Through intention, though, you can access the unconditional acceptance and Love which takes away fear, anger, shame, guilt, grief, or any others source of distress. You can experience inspiration and allow your energy to shift with a resulting shift in any emotion, belief, or memory that causes you distress. Without intention you engage in the work of striving to change and grow by force of will.

Living with intention is about spirit, releasing and allowing. Living without intention is about ego, forcing and doing.

Intention is humility and alignment.

To echo the writings of Wayne Dyer and other spiritual teachers, the only thing that separates us from Source, from Love, is the belief that we are separate from it. And because all beliefs are learned, we can each choose to benefit from believing that there is a Source of pure Love which we can tap in to, or we can choose to believe we are separate from any divine Source and continue to rely on willpower and strive for serenity.

## Wrap Up

As we bring this chapter to a close, you can see the importance of making a conscious choice to live with a 3D perception of yourself. It is in your self-interest to understand that you were unconsciously conditioned into accepting a 2D view of life, a paradigm that focuses on matter, and can now consciously choose to live from a 3D paradigm, one that focuses on energy and allowing Loving energy to support you.

When you see yourself as a dynamic interplay of three components, mind, body, energy, with energy being fundamental to all three, then you realize that you can impact your mind and body by addressing the energy system. Imagine how much more effective your self-help activities will be when you are intentionally using your energy system to improve your well-being! You can do it.

Realizing that you can shift your energy and shift emotions, beliefs, and memories that rob you of serenity, is a basis for hope.

Remember, traditional self-help works primarily through the mind and body. Working this way is all good, but we can enhance and complete the intervention process by working through the energy system as well. This becomes self-help for the 21st century... enlightened self-help.

By embracing a 3D approach, we are taking a complete understanding of the dynamic interplay of systems within the human being, and using all of the resources that are available to us to support our mind, body, and energy systems - in order to create the shift we desire so that we can move forward and grow in our life with greater ease and enjoy more peace, serenity, and joy.

The 3D Perception Diagram provides you with a way of understanding the dynamics that are at play; and seeing that you can use your energy system to give you a renewed sense of hope. As you work through these new ideas, you are gaining a new understanding and a way to approach those issues which seemed unsolvable to you, issues you felt stuck with and trapped by.

Okay. We have done some science, we have looked at one spiritual truth, now let's look at how tapping into the energy of pure Love can help you to shift emotions, beliefs, and memories which cause you distress, allowing you to move forward with greater ease.

## Resources

David Feinstein, Ph.D., Donna Eden and Gary Craig, *The Promise of Energy Psychology: Revolutionary Tools for Dramatic Personal Change* (New York: Penguin Books, 2005)

David R. Hawkins, M.D, Ph.D., *Power vs. Force: The Hidden Determinants of Human Behavior* (Carlsbad, CA: Hay House, 2002)

Donna Eden: www.edenenergymedicine.com

William James, *The Varieties of Religious Experience* (New York: Penguin Books, 1982)

# Chapter 6

# The Belief Tree

*I*n 2010 I had been studying energy psychology for 6 years and working with clients for most of that time. That experience made two phenomena jump out to me. One, it was clear that energy techniques helped people to remove behaviors, emotions, beliefs, and memories that caused them distress. Second, it was also clear that most of the people I worked with felt overwhelmed by what was challenging them and had trouble breaking their challenges down into bite size pieces. I really wanted an easier way to help people break down a problem into smaller, more understandable and manageable parts.

That's when the image of the Belief Tree popped into my awareness. We have a large oak tree that shades part of our backyard and I always enjoy sitting under that tree. One day I was looking at the tree and it struck me that the tree was a metaphor for how behaviors, emotions, beliefs, memories, and energy all fit together. That "aha" and some help from a graphic designer led to the Belief Tree illustration. These ideas can help you to feel less overwhelmed by a problem and to begin making progress in finding a resolution, just as it has for me and many others.

The basic premise behind the Belief Tree is that we each have a collection of memories, beliefs, emotions, and behaviors which are unique to us and are an expression of our personal energy system.

This collection represents your own, personal belief tree. When you are able to put these elements into an understandable model or illustration, and see their relationship to your energy system, it's much easier to understand the connections between them and how you can effect change within your life using the technique I will be sharing with you in the next section of this book.

Let's start by taking a look at the Belief Tree illustration on the following page. As in the prior two chapters, I will walk you through each component of the illustration just as I did with the 2D and 3D Perception Diagrams.

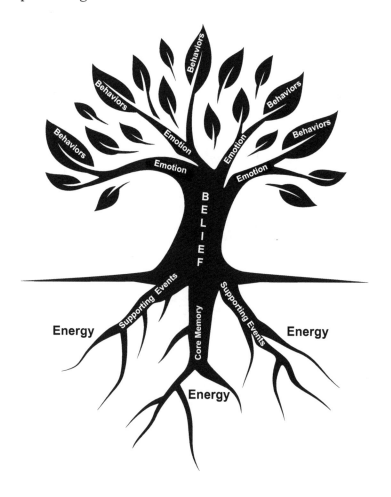

## Behaviors

Starting at the very top, with the leaves on the tree, you can see that the leaves represent behaviors. That's because behaviors are really just what's on the surface. They are the tip of the iceberg, if you will. Behaviors are the expression of an emotion - they are putting physical form into what it is that you are feeling.

If you're feeling happy, you act happy. If you're feeling sad, you act sad. If you're feeling angry, you act angry, and so on. Behind any behavior, there is an emotion. It may be ambivalence, it may be indifference, but there's still some emotion that is underlying any behavior. In terms of practical application, when working with folks, I typically ask them, "What is the behavior that's bothering you?" They will tell me and then I'll say, "What are you feeling when you do that?" Immediately, we're able to get to the emotion that's underlying the behavior. We are able to use the behavior as an indicator pointing toward an underlying emotion.

Now, on occasion, people are not able to tell me what the emotion is that's behind the behavior. They're just doing it, it's unconscious. This often shows up when I am helping someone that is trying to lose weight but find themselves eating unconsciously. They are not in touch with why they are eating. That's fine; we start there. If all they know is that this is a behavior that is bothering them, then we'll take the Pondera Process® and apply it to that behavior, knowing that the Process is going to help them to get in touch with what they're feeling. It is that feeling, that emotion, which is driving the behavior.

One of my clients, Dianne, was frustrated because her weight had gotten far above her preferred level, and she found herself eating almost continually when she was home. She knew that she wasn't hungry, but felt herself compelled to eat, anyway. Dianne is a very insightful person, but she could not figure out why she was eating like that.

Together, we took a 3D approach to the situation and used the Pondera Process® to help balance the energy around the behavior. By taking an energy approach, Dianne was quickly able to relax about this challenging behavior.

As is often the case, when we can turn down the emotions of an immediate situation, we can then think a bit more clearly and gain some insight. This was true for Dianne. After using a 3D approach to bring down the intensity of her emotions, I asked her what, if anything, had changed in her life at around the same time as her eating behavior changed. A light bulb lit up for her.

Dianne had always led an active life. She worked about 30 hours a week, was actively engaged with her grandchildren, and enjoyed hiking and bicycling. About 18 months prior to our conversation, Dianne had hip replacement surgery. Needless to say, that slowed her down and meant a lot more time spent at home. Then she had a second hip replacement, which meant even more down time.

What Dianne realized during our conversation was that being slowed down during her recuperation and having to spend more time at home had led her to start eating out of boredom. This is not unusual. Much unwanted eating is a compensation for something we are feeling.

But wait, she had completely recovered from the hip surgeries, so why was she still eating unconsciously? Dianne then realized that she had emotionally connected being at home with being bored and eating during her recovery. Even though she was back to hiking with her grandchildren, when she went home the setting triggered a feeling of boredom and an unconscious desire to eat as a way of compensating.

Once Dianne had received this insight, she was able to take concrete steps to improve her emotional well-being. She was able to see what had been an unconscious connection between a feeling of boredom and eating. She was able to use a 3D approach to address the feeling of boredom and the unconscious connection between what she was feeling and being at home, which had carried over from recuperation. This, in turn, helped her to change her behavior. Note that when we started our conversation, Dianne did not know why she was doing what she was doing. By using the Pondera Process® to balance the energy around the behavior, she was able to tap into the underlying dynamics and regain a sense of hope that she wasn't trapped in an unwanted behavior.

As an aside, this conversation and realization by Dianne took less than an hour. Using a 3D approach and understanding that there was an energy component to the dilemma, made gaining insight much quicker than with more traditional, 2D approaches.

Many traditional self-help techniques stop at this level of understanding. Their focus is on unwanted behaviors and their intervention at the behavioral level. For example, they recommend snapping a rubber band on your wrist whenever you engage in an unwanted behavior. Or they suggest putting your hand up and emphatically saying "STOP" whenever you have an unwanted thought. These practices come out of a behavioristic approach toward human behavior which was pioneered by B.F. Skinner. While these practices can be helpful, they come from a 2D understanding of human behavior and are limited in their effectiveness.

By having a 3D understanding and approach to human behavior we can enjoy significantly improved results, just as Dianne did.

## Emotions

Going back to the Belief Tree diagram, you'll see that emotions are the branches which support the behaviors, which are the leaves. That is because, as we said before, behaviors are just an expression of emotions. So, the emotions are supporting the behaviors, just as branches are supporting the leaves.

Emotions have two dimensions to them, as we saw in the 3D Perception Diagram. There is a physical or chemical aspect to emotions, and there's also an energy component to them. We know that we feel emotions due to the release of chemicals from the brain into the bloodstream, which we then feel in our muscles and in different organs. We can feel the emotions through a quickened pulse, through our rate of breathing, through the tension felt in different muscles and other physical sensations.

There's also an energy dimension to emotions. The word "emotion" is derived from the Latin verb "emovere" which means "to move". So, the word "emotion" can literally be understood as "energy in motion". As illustrated in the 3D Perception Diagram, you first perceive an event which then impacts your energy system. This perception causes a disruption in your energy system, which triggers the brain to release chemicals, which you then feel as an emotion. While it's natural to think that the emotion is just a physical sensation because you are feeling it, at its heart, at its foundation, it's really a disruption in the energy system. It's the disruption of the energy system that you're feeling because of the biological process. Think about when you feel stressed or anxious. Your breathing becomes shallower, your pulse quickens, you feel yourself tense up, and thoughts start running uncontrollably through your head. When you are experiencing all of these sensations, it's natural to think stress is a physical sensation when, fundamentally, it's a disruption in your energy system which you are feeling physically.

Understanding that there is an energy dimension to emotions was critical to my making progress with my anger issues. This understanding helped me to stop being so judgmental of myself, being angry at myself, when I acted out of unhealthy anger. This understanding helped me to get underneath what I was feeling and to begin a healing process at the source of the problem. By understanding that there was an energy dynamic underlying my anger, I no longer expected myself to manage my feelings and behavior by willpower alone. An expectation I failed at most of the time and then berated myself for. By understanding that there was an energy dynamic at work, I was able to address the feelings and behavior at that more fundamental level. The result was a lot more compassion and patience with myself and much quicker progress in replacing anger with increased serenity.

For example, I often felt anger when I perceived that someone wasn't listening to what I was saying. I instinctively took it as a personal affront and the anger kicked in. I could feel my jaw tighten, my shoulders become tense, the rush of adrenaline, my blood pressure go up… all those sensations common to feeling angry.

I used to feel trapped in my anger. It was my protection from being further hurt, but that protection came at a high price. I tried many traditional approaches to anger management which resulted in limited success. However, when I took a 3D approach to my anger and saw it as a disruption in my energy system, then I was able to use the Pondera Process® and balance the energy around what I was feeling. This approach helped me to process the emotion much more quickly and avoid behavior I would regret later. I was able to respond, rather than react, when I started to feel angry.

More importantly, though, is that by no longer feeling trapped in my anger -- trapped in my emotion -- I could begin to see how I was perceiving the situation. I was able to step outside of my anger and begin to see the beliefs that led me to feeling personally affronted and becoming angry. Now I could start the healing process at a more fundamental level and begin to remove the sources of my unhealthy anger. This leads us to the next part of the Belief Tree.

## Beliefs

You will notice that the trunk of the tree says Beliefs. It is your beliefs which result in your emotions, just as the trunk of tree supports the branches. When you change the way you perceive an event, when you change the beliefs through which you filter the event, you change your emotional response to the event. Let me recap a few key points about beliefs which we looked at in more depth with the 2D Perception Diagram:

- Beliefs are the rules of life that we've taken on
- Beliefs are both conscious and unconscious
- All beliefs are learned
- Beliefs are not predetermined
- Beliefs are not genetic
- Beliefs do not have to be permanent
- We are not branded by our beliefs
- Beliefs are optional, we get to choose them
- We can unlearn old limiting beliefs and we can choose to take on new empowering beliefs. It's an option that's always available to us.

We learned our beliefs from people that are significant to us, we learned them from significant events in our life, and we learned them from the communities that we were part of. They were all designed to help us to feel and stay safe. Whether it be physically safe or emotionally safe, we still took on those beliefs that facilitated us feeling safe at that time and place in our life. We are then inclined to filter information and experiences in a manner that confirms and reinforces our beliefs.

You can see the importance of beliefs in what has been called the "twin study," where researchers took identical twins who were separated at birth and tracked the quality of their life over several decades. What they found is that identical twins, children who had identical DNA, children who had an identical genetic predisposition, experienced a very different quality of life. Researchers found that much of the difference in the quality of life experienced by each of the twins depended on their belief structure. A large factor in their respective lives depended on the amount of stress that each experienced during their lifetime. The different beliefs that each of the twins took on, which contributed to the amount of stress they experienced, impacted not only the quality of their health, but the longevity of their life. The study provides clear evidence of the power of the beliefs that we take on and how they can impact us physically.

As you can see on the Belief Tree diagram, just as the trunk of the tree supports the branches which supports the leaves, the beliefs that we learn lead to the emotions that we feel, which in turn leads to the behaviors that we exhibit. Beliefs are a filter, as illustrated in the 2D & 3D Perception Diagrams from the previous chapters. It follows from this understanding that if we shift a belief, then we are able to shift the emotion connected to that belief because we will be perceiving an event differently. When we feel differently, we're able to act differently. This is an important understanding to take hold of. There is a tremendous sense of liberation and hope that comes from knowing you have the ability to discard old, limiting beliefs and to choose new beliefs which empower you and bring you greater serenity.

In your personal journey, you are going to start where you find yourself now and with what you are aware of at this moment. You can start with any behavior or emotion which is causing you distress. But eventually, you want to get down to the underlying belief which is coloring how you perceive events, how you feel and how you behave. You want to get to the belief, the rule of life that you have learned. You want to see if there is a new, more empowering belief which will serve you better that you can make your own.

Now, if you were to come at this process from a conventional psychology or traditional self-help approach, you would likely use an approach such as Cognitive Behavior Therapy, which says that it takes 21 days to shift a behavior. It has been my experience, and the experience of many others, using energy tools like the Pondera

Process® and others, that you can often shift a behavior in 21 minutes. It doesn't have to take 21 days to change a behavior. If you understand the energetic dimension to a behavior, if you take steps to shift the energy of the underlying emotion and belief, you can realize progress much faster and with greater ease. If you address this dynamic change process at the energetic level and shift the energy around a belief, you can then feel better, which then empowers you to behave and act better.

This understanding about beliefs, and how they are connected to my emotions and behaviors, was very helpful in moving past my ODSR (overdeveloped sense of responsibility). It helped me to put the pieces of my emotional jigsaw together so that I had a clearer picture of what was happening in my life. That clearer picture, in turn, made it easier for me to take constructive steps which would bring greater serenity into my life.

Understanding that beliefs are learned and have an energy component to them, I knew that I could use the Pondera Process® to balance the energy around my ODSR and free myself from that limiting belief. I could free myself up to learn a more empowering belief, a more empowering rule of life.

Using a 3D approach toward a limiting belief, a belief that limited the serenity in my life, expedited my being able to move past my ODSR. By balancing the energy around my old belief, I was able to release it and become able to take on a more empowering belief. I was able to replace my old belief with the empowering belief that we are each responsible for our own happiness. I was no longer responsible for everyone else's happiness.

But to completely let go of that limiting belief of ODSR I had to also look at the memories which had taught me that limiting belief in the first place. Taking the time and having the intention to balance the energy around the limiting belief made it much easier for me to feel safe in recalling the key memories that had taught me the limiting belief initially.

# Memory

Looking again at the Belief Tree diagram, you'll see that the roots of the tree are labeled "core memory". In my work with hundreds of people, I have seen that it's actually memories that are the root of all beliefs. Memories are our recollection of a past event, where we learned a particular belief or had a current belief reinforced at that point in time.

Now, oftentimes people aren't able to get to the underlying memory of a belief. That's not a problem. Lots of folks have been able to realize the progress they were seeking and the results they desired by using the Pondera Process® at the emotional and belief levels. It is desirable, but not necessary, to address the memory(s) underlying a belief in order to see progress and experience greater serenity. It is not essential for them to identify where they learned a particular belief that no longer serves what is highest and best for them. They are still able to realize the progress that they are seeking and the result that they desire.

Let me talk a little bit about the role of memories here and some aspects of them. The first thing I would note is that a memory is your interpretation of events that took place at a particular time and place. A memory, again, just like a belief, is not determined. It's not set in stone. A memory is your *interpretation* of events at the time they took place not necessarily what actually happened. Your memory and interpretation of past events does not change over time without a conscious intention to reframe how you see the past event, to see the event differently. So, if you took on a fear at the age of six because of something that happened to you, when you reflect on that memory now you are likely still interpreting it as a six-year-old. That memory, and the impact of that memory on your energy system, remains the same unless you take steps to shift the energy around that memory and reframe the past event in light of your understanding of the event from your present point of view.

Let me give you an example. My dad had just turned 20 when I was born. Needless to say, in my early years I was being raised by a man who was still growing up himself. I had a lot of resentment over many of the things I experienced with my dad and my anger had a negative effect on my life for many years. It wasn't until I started doing energy work around my feelings that it dawned on me that he was *only* 20 years old. What kind of father would I have been at 20? Suddenly I was able to see my father in a new light, not as a 7-year-old, but as a father myself who can appreciate what that 20-year-old was able to do given his age and his own upbringing. By using energy tools to shift the energy around old emotions and memories, I was able to see my father differently; take on a more mature, empowered understanding of what happened in my past and begin the forgiveness process.

The second thing I would note about memories is that they can be shifted the same way beliefs can be shifted. In psychology this is known as "reframing", the ability to look at an old event in a new way. My ability to interpret childhood memories of experiences with my father is an example of reframing. Or you may remember falling out of a tree, so you became afraid of heights. But as you age and look at that past experience, you have the ability to say, "Oh, no, I can climb a tree because I'm larger and stronger. I know why I slipped and I'm not going to do it again." So now it's safe to climb a tree. Or perhaps as a child you were afraid of water and you didn't want to learn how to swim. As an adult, you are able to move slowly into the water, become more comfortable, feel safe, and now you're able to enjoy the water and you're able to swim.

Third, along with the awareness that memories and beliefs can be shifted is the understanding that there is more than one interpretation possible for any particular event. Your memory is the interpretation that you took on at that time and place and which was then downloaded into your memory banks. It is the interpretation that you felt would keep you safe at that time. What's important to understand is by using energy tools like the Pondera Process®, you don't have to hold onto old interpretations of past events in order to feel safe. You now have the ability to feel safe while updating your understanding of old events and replacing any limiting belief(s) which came from your previous understanding. You can safely change memories and beliefs that are no longer serving you.

You have the opportunity to connect with the Divine, to connect with a Higher Power, to the Source of Love and loving energy, so that you feel safe letting go of a belief or a memory that you formed earlier in life. When you are able to reframe an event, the memory becomes like a bee sting. You remember being stung by a bee but the pain of the sting doesn't interfere with your life now. That's what you have the ability to do when you balance the energy around an old memory and take the emotional charge out of them. The Pondera Process® can help you to take that sting, or take that charge, out of old painful memories.

Again, I would note that it's not critical that you recall the memory of where you took on a belief. We're going to start at the surface. We're going to start with what your behavior is and move down your belief tree to identify what is beneath the surface. If you're able to identify the emotions underneath the behavior, do the Pondera Process® for Emotions. If beneath the emotion you're able to say, "Well, this is the rule of life that I learned, this is the belief I learned which led to this emotion," then do the Pondera Process® for Beliefs. You can shift the energy around that belief and take on a new, more empowering belief to help you. If you're able to say, "Well, I know where I learned that belief, it came from this memory," and reframing that memory would help you to move forward, then do the Pondera Process® for Memories. Shift the energy around that memory so that you can interpret events differently, which in turn helps you to take on a new more empowering belief, which then leads to more affirming emotions and to the behavior that you desire.

## Supporting Events

You will also notice on the Belief Tree diagram that there are side roots coming off the core memory that I've labeled "supporting events." That is simply to illustrate that you have secondary or supporting life events that reinforce a core memory. It's similar to beliefs: you have a core belief and then you filter the information and events around you in order to support that belief. The same thing is happening here. If you had a fear of heights, from something that happened to you as a child, then that fear leads you to make subsequent choices where you avoid heights in order to feel safe. These secondary experiences do not have the same emotional and energetic impact of the original experience, but they do reinforce the original memory. Then, when you look back on your life, and find yourself saying, "Well, yes, I am afraid of heights because I remember this, I remember this, and I remember this."

These are all just supporting events or supporting memories that reinforce the core memory. As you shift the energy around these supporting events or supporting memories - and then eventually get to the core memory - you'll be able to shift the memory itself. You'll be able to reinterpret that initial life event or experience, and take from it a more empowering understanding or belief that will help you to move forward with much more joy, peace, and serenity in your life.

## Energy

The last element on the Belief Tree illustration is "energy." You'll notice that the tree is planted into the ground or soil. The soil represents the energy that surrounds your tree, the energy you are pulling into your life, into your own belief tree. It is helpful to see your life as being a tree, as a compilation of behaviors, emotions, beliefs, and memories.... all of which are pulling energy into your life.

Remember, everything is a form of energy. Every behavior, emotion, belief, and memory has an energy signature, and each of them pulls energy similar to it from your environment. That's, in part, why it has been hard to change unwanted elements in your life where you haven't used intention to intervene at the energy level of the challenge. Each element of your belief tree looks for similar energy in your environment to feed off of and resists 2D efforts to change them. A more effective way to change unwanted elements in your life is to approach them from a 3D perspective as we have discussed. When you intentionally bring in positive, high vibration, Loving energy into your personal energy system you are able to change the energy of an unwanted behavior, emotion, belief, or memory, you are able to change the item itself. You are able to change an unwanted behavior, emotion, belief, or memory which currently limits your serenity into one that serves what is highest and best for you.

Rest assured, I will show you a way to do this easily and effectively.

Now, there are two types of energy: energy that empowers and energy that disempowers. Empowering energy is balanced, harmonious, flows smoothly, and brings greater serenity into your life. Disempowering energy creates disruptions within your energy system by causing it to be scattered and chaotic, as in when you feel anxious, or by causing blockages within your energy system which feels heavy, as in when you feel depressed.

The important point to understand, as I mentioned at the start of this chapter, is that we each have a belief tree which represents our life. It is the collection of memories, beliefs, emotions, and behaviors and energy that are unique to us. And each of our belief trees pulls from our environments the energy that is similar to it. If you have a limiting belief, then you will unconsciously seek out and attract energy from your environment that matches your emotional state at this moment. You unconsciously seek the type of energy that you are familiar and comfortable with, whether that energy be chaotic or balanced and harmonious.

As you choose to use your intention to shift those limiting emotions, beliefs, and memories and the energy around them in a way that is highest and best for you, you will also change the type of energy that you unconsciously pull into your life. Essentially, you are shifting the energy around an emotion, belief, or memory and balancing it by intentionally bringing in more light and more loving energy. As you can see, as a result of intentionally changing your belief tree, you will start to unconsciously draw in more Love and more light into your life. For me, in my own journey, as I became more intentional about shifting the energy around my anger and limiting beliefs like my ODSR, I unconsciously started to draw into my life more and more positive energy from the people and events in my life which resulted in a much greater sense of serenity. I attracted people who had more of a positive energy to them and opportunities to grow and develop in a healthier way.

Remember that energy is fundamental to everything. It's the soil from which our trees grow. That energy can either be positive, balanced, harmonious, and empowering or it can be disruptive and disempowering. This energy feeds your memories, your beliefs, your emotions, and your behaviors. As you shift the energy around anyone of these four components, then you shift that item itself and change the type of energy it pulls into your life. It gives us a tremendous amount of freedom and a tremendous amount of hope to know that we can work within our energy system, in connecting to the Loving energy that is fundamental to our universe, in order to create those shifts and to help ourselves move forward with much greater ease.

## My Journey

I have found the Belief Tree to be a very helpful illustration for myself and for those I have taught. It has, as I indicated earlier, helped me to sort out the jigsaw puzzle of different feelings and thoughts in any area of life where I or one of my clients has felt distress.

For me, this illustration helped to put my challenges with anger (an emotion) and my ODSR (a belief) into a larger context. It helped me to see the dynamics at work and how all of the pieces fit together. This clarity, in turn, made it easier for me to break down these two challenges into smaller pieces and helped me to see a path forward. By the way, it has also helped me with a lot of other life challenges beyond the two I have been sharing about in this book.

Let me share with you one more metaphor to illustrate how there can be different levels of disruption for any given problem.

Imagine that you bumped into something or have fallen and received a bruise on your body. This is a common occurrence and the bruise will go away on its own with the passage of time. This is a bruise on your body, your physical self. We can call this a physical bruise.

Similarly, we all have had experiences that upset us emotionally, but not physically. These are bruises to our emotions and to our minds. In many instances these will fade away with time or through familiar practices like prayer, journaling, or talking to a friend. These can be called emotional bruises.

Then there is a third, deeper level of our self that can be bruised and that is our energy system. These are hurts that are so emotionally charged that they bruise us at a deeper level. It is at this level of our being that those stubborn problems live. Let's call these energy bruises. These are problems that don't seem to respond well to conventional interventions.

The good news is that we can access the Loving energy of a Higher Power to heal these bruises to our energy system. Just as acupuncture can be used to restore the normal flow of energy to aid physical healing, so 3D techniques allow us to restore balance and harmony when our energy system has been deeply bruised.

While traditional self-help and other 2D techniques have helped me with some of my emotional bruises, it took a 3D approach to bring relief and resolution to my energy bruises.

In addressing my anger and ODSR challenges, I started at the level of my awareness. Whether it was my behavior, what I was feeling, a belief that I was aware of, or a memory that I sensed was the place that a particular limiting belief had taken root - that is where I started. As I used energy techniques such as the Pondera Process® appropriate to the level of my awareness, I received further insight and understanding of where my distress was originating. Then, as I took steps to balance the energy at each level, I gained a freedom to shift my memories, beliefs, feelings, and behaviors. I moved toward a place that was highest and best for me. I gained a freedom to shift toward a place that gave me greater serenity. I was able to change my personal Belief Tree so that it bore even sweeter fruit.

Let me close this chapter on the Belief Tree by emphasizing and encouraging you to start at the level of your awareness. If you are aware of the behavior that you no longer desire, then work at that level. If you understand the emotion that's driving that behavior, then work at that level. If you understand the belief that is underlying the emotions, go there. If you know the memory where this underlying belief began then start there. The point is that you start at the level of your awareness.

You can use an energy technique such as the Pondera Process® for each of these levels - for behaviors, emotions, beliefs, and memories. Start with where you are. Start with the level of your awareness.

# Resources

Pondera Process for Emotions www.rebuildingafter.com/pondera-process-for-emotions-audio/

Pondera Process for Beliefs www.rebuildingafter.com/pondera-process-for-beliefs-audio/

# Part 3

## Journey Forward

# Chapter 7

# The Pondera Process® for Stress

N ow that we have spent some time understanding the difference between a 2D traditional approach to self-help (Chapter 4) and a more empowering 3D approach to self-help (Chapter 5) in general, and stress in particular, we are ready to look at a practical application of the 3D approach. In this chapter I will give you an overview of the Pondera Process® (Process), describe some of the key concepts that make the Process effective, and provide you with the step-by-step Pondera Process® for Stress.

## The Backstory of the Pondera Process®

You may recall from the Introduction, that in 2004 I was introduced to neuro-linguistic programming (NLP) while taking a "Skyrocket Your Sales" class. It was through my training in NLP that I began learning about quantum physics and began to realize that everything is a form of energy. I also came to understand that when you shift the energy around an item, such as an emotion, you change the item itself. It turned out that NLP is one of many techniques that can be used to shift the energy around something causing you distress.

As I read and studied about working with our personal energy system in order to facilitate personal growth, I was introduced to the Emotional Freedom Technique (EFT). This was in 2005 and I first learned of EFT from a cassette recording (remember those?) by Dr. Lee Pulos. While NLP is effective, and many people prefer this technique over other alternatives, I found EFT to be easier to implement for the general population. So, I became trained to an advanced level of competency in EFT.

My exposure to other people practicing EFT then led me to learn about the larger field of energy psychology and the Association for Comprehensive Energy Psychology (ACEP), an association of hundreds of practitioners using a variety of energy techniques to help others. Being involved in ACEP introduced me to a wealth of information, both theoretical and practical, which deepened my understanding of how to work with our energy system to effect desired changes.

Naturally, as I was learning all of this fun information, I started trying it out on myself and any willing friends or family members. As I saw the positive results they were experiencing, I became even more confident in the effectiveness of a 3D approach to life's challenges.

Then, somewhere around 2007, I had an opportunity to begin working with individuals who were in recovery from addiction to drugs. Given how my life had been significantly affected by addiction, I jumped in with both feet.

Since I was working with the many issues surrounding addiction, I read *Alcoholics Anonymous* a couple of times. However, while I was interested in learning the 12 Steps of AA, I was equally interested in understanding why the 12 Step process worked. What were the concepts, insights, and understandings within the 12 Step process that made it effective for many, many people? In addition, I wondered if EFT or other techniques from energy psychology would complement the 12 Step process. These questions led to much more reading, conversations, and reflection.

Against this backdrop, I was also encountering a practical problem. I was primarily teaching EFT during this time. Now, as a technique, EFT has you tap on your body's meridian points while saying a variety of statements. The technique worked, but I kept encountering resistance from clients and students to the idea of tapping on the meridian points. Tapping on different points on their body just felt odd. Since I didn't have a more effective way to help them to let go of their distress, I spent a lot of time encouraging people to focus on the benefits that they were receiving rather than on the unusual technique. Nevertheless, I was open to finding a technique that was more user friendly while equally effective.

In 2014, I was at an ACEP conference and attended a class by Dr. John Diepold where he was teaching his Heart Assisted Therapy (HAT) technique. Instead of tapping on the meridian points, Dr. Diepold had individuals place their hands over their heart while repeating a series of specific statements. I recall him showing a picture of a woman who was overcome by a feeling of joy and how she instinctively brought both hands up to her heart. This was a much more "natural" action than tapping on the meridian points. I instantly knew that this was at least a partial answer to the challenge of making a 3D approach to life's challenges more user friendly.

During the summer of 2014, I continued to mull over these crosscurrents of ideas. It was from within this dynamic mix of ideas that the Pondera Process® emerged. I took some of the best elements from the 12 Steps, from EFT, other energy techniques, and put them into a more user-friendly process. Then it was a matter of trial and error, first on myself, then on friends and family, then on the community at large… anyone who was willing to try a new solution to old problems. Through the feedback from others and observing which elements of the Process consistently provided positive results, I refined the Process into its current form.

## Going a Little Deeper: Why Pondera?

So why is it called Pondera? This process works because it balances the energy around an item (e.g., behavior, emotion, belief, or memory) which has been creating an imbalance in a person's energy system, and this often results in a feeling of distress. As I was coming up with a name for this process, I realized I was looking for a word for balance to get to the core meaning of the process. As I reflected on the idea of getting to the root cause and core of the process it led me to the idea that Latin contains the root for our English language (as well as others) and I looked up the Latin word for balance. As you may have guessed, the Latin word for balance is pondera. I thought, "Hmm, Pondera Process® -- that has a nice alliteration to it – so, let's go with that name." Yes, it is unusual, but it is also accurate. Hopefully, as more and more people give it a try and benefit from the Process, "pondera" will become a familiar word.

When asked to describe the Pondera Process® (Process), I typically say something along the lines of it being an energy technique which combines current scientific understandings, psychological principles, and timeless spiritual truths in a user-friendly manner. The Process teaches the individual how to balance the energy around that which is causing them distress. This balancing of the energy makes it easier for the person to gain a sense of serenity and clarity. This, in turn, makes it easier for the person to grow through and resolve a given life challenge that has been causing them distress, often for a long time.

A distinctive feature of the Pondera Process® is that it uses your heart center to effect change. It is also a process which you can easily do on your own. Again, there are many different energy techniques available, and to the extent they help balance and harmonize your personal energy system, they are helpful. While these techniques are helpful, many of them require another person to assist you, and/ or they feel awkward to use at times. My goal with the Pondera

Process® is for you to be able to simply and comfortably use the Process to help yourself.

You can think of the different energy techniques as being flavors of ice cream. You get to sample different techniques and choose the one that appeals to you the most. The Pondera Process® is one additional tasty flavor.

In addition to ease of use, by focusing on the heart, I have found that the majority of my clients get to the core elements of what is challenging them and are able to realize results faster. My hunch is that the heart acts like the motherboard of our energy system. Just as the motherboard is the central communications point through which all elements of a computer connect, so the heart is the central communications point through which the energy in all parts of your being are connected. When we effect change through the heart, all parts of our being can receive the benefits.

The effectiveness of the Process is further enhanced when you use the Belief Tree (Chapter 6) to guide your activity. It can help you to stay out of the weeds and focus on the primary source of your distress.

Okay. Now that you have an idea of how the Pondera Process® evolved, and why I consider it to be a valuable addition to the self-help field, we can get down to the particulars.

In the rest of this chapter, I will walk you through how to use the Pondera Process® for Stress. By the end of this chapter, you will have an energy technique which you can use on your own or with others and which has consistently been effective for countless individuals since 2014.

## Using the Pondera Process® for Stress

Let's start by turning to the end of this chapter where you will see the three pages that make up the Pondera Process® for Stress. You will notice that there is the Pondera Process® for Stress itself, then there is an Instructions sheet and an Inventory sheet. In order to keep things simple, I am going to walk you through the content of the Pondera Process® for Stress and summarize the key points from the other two pages. You can always refer back to the Instructions page for more information on how to use the Process for Stress.

To the above point, I need to explain four items in the Process for Stress before we jump in.

## Using the Healthy Heart Hold

Take a look at Step 3 and you will see where I refer to the Healthy Heart Hold. The what?! Relax, this is just a term I came up with to describe placing both of your hands over your heart, one on top of the other. Imagine a person who is surprised by unexpected joy and instinctively puts both of their hands over their heart. That is what we're calling the Healthy Heart Hold.

It doesn't matter which hand is on top. You will be keeping both hands over your heart as you go through all nine statements in the Stress script.

## Take 3 deep breaths, switch your hands and take 3 more deep breaths

Looking again at Step 3, you will notice that after you say each of the nine statements in Step 3, I ask you to take 3 deep breaths, switch hands and take 3 more deep breaths. Huh?

I have observed over the years that a particular way of breathing increases the effectiveness of the Process. When you take a breath, breathe in through your nose, filling up your stomach like a balloon, then slowly exhale through your mouth.

The instruction to breathe in through your nose and out through your mouth is pretty straightforward. Will the Process work if you don't breathe this way, or if you only do it some of the time? Yes.

This breathing technique that I am suggesting is common to many spiritual practices. While it is not essential, it does improve the results you will receive from the Process.

What is important about the way you breathe is that you take deep breaths. When you breathe deeply, you will notice that your stomach fills up like a balloon. I want you to inhale as much Love, light, and positive energy as you can while doing the statements - so breathe deeply!

After taking 3 deep breaths, I ask you to switch hands and take 3 more deep breaths. In the end, you will take a total of 6 breaths for each statement.

This part is important. Switching your hands helps the statements to be received by both parts of your brain - the left side and the right side. The neurophysiology of this is outside of the scope of this book, but it is important. We have experimented with going through each statement and not switching hands. Those results were consistently inferior to when the hands were switched.

So, take 3 deep breaths, switch hands, and take 3 more deep breaths after each statement.

**Fill in the blanks**

Looking at Step 3 of the Pondera Process® for Stress page, you will notice that there are blanks in statements 2, 5 and 9. You will need to decide how to fill these in before actually going through the Process. Statement 2 of the Stress script is straightforward. It asks you to identify where in your body you are feeling the stress. I elaborate on this a bit more in Step 1 below.

Now take a look at Statements 5 and 9 of the Stress script. This is where you will choose a term or phrase with which you are comfortable and which refers to that which is greater than yourself, that which is a source of Love for you. What are you comfortable with calling the Loving energy which is available to all of us and which you can access through your intention?

I have inserted the term "Higher Power" in the blank, but this is only a suggestion. Students and clients of mine often use the terms God, Source, Universe, Nature, and other terms that have meaning to them. Simply choose a term or phrase that you are comfortable saying. There is no right or wrong language for you to use, only that which has meaning for you. Any language you use in referring to the eternal Loving energy that is fundamental to our world will work.

**Say each statement out loud**

Read the first statement in the Stress script, out loud, and take 3 deep breaths.

Whenever possible, it is preferable to read each statement out loud. Will the Process work if you say the statements silently? Yes. Does the Process have a stronger effect on you when you say the statements out loud? Definitely.

By saying the statement out loud, you are getting it out of your head and making it more of an objective statement. Also, by saying it out loud you will hear the words in your own voice, which aids you in feeling safe and accepting of the statement.

So, whenever possible, say each statement out loud. The louder the better.

O.K. Now that we have the preliminaries out of the way, let's go through each step in the Pondera Process® for Stress!

# Step 1

**Notice what is causing you stress and where you are feeling stress in your body. It is preferable that you write this down on the Inventory sheet.**

It makes sense to start at the beginning, by identifying to the best of your ability what is causing you to feel stressed and where this stress is emerging in your body. Frequently there are multiple things which contribute to our feeling stressed, however it is most effective to break down the stress puzzle into individual pieces and to balance the energy around each piece. By breaking down stress into bite-sized pieces, it is much more manageable and in due course the overall picture will be one of greater serenity.

Where you are feeling a particular stress in your body. Is it in your shoulders? Lower back? Stomach? Head or neck?

Don't skip this step and say, "I just feel stressed." The more you can tune into your body and identify what you feel and where you feel it, the more effective the Process will be.

Now, look at the Inventory sheet and write down in the "event" column *what* specific or particular thing is causing you stress; and write in the fourth column *where* in your body you are feeling the stress in your body.

A quick note about using the Inventory sheet. While it is not essential to write down what you are observing and experiencing when doing the Process, it is highly desirable. I and others have used this Process in situations where we couldn't write things down, and the stress we were feeling was still reduced. However, it is preferable to write it down, especially when you are just starting out using the Pondera Process®.

There are several benefits to writing down what you are experiencing. First, as I mentioned before, it helps you to get out of your head and into your body - which helps to make the Process more effective.

Second, it allows you to cut through the confusion of stress and to gain insights into what you can do to improve a particular situation.

Third, when you are starting out with the Process you are likely to be surprised by how well it works - how it helps you to feel better. Your brain will then try to find reasons other than using the Pondera Process® for why you feel better. This is common and normal. After all, for most people, this is a very different approach to relieving stress and it's a challenge to bring something so novel into your thinking. By writing down what you are experiencing, you will have objective proof that this change in your approach to Stress is helping you. And, as you repeat the Process for a variety of stressful events, you will see a pattern of effectiveness and it will be easier for your brain to accept the Pondera Process® as a positive part of your life.

Okay. You have written down the event that is causing you stress and where in your body you are feeling the stress. Let's move on.

## Step 2

**Rate the intensity of the stress you are feeling on a scale of 0 - 10 (with 0 being not at all and 10 being the worst it has ever been) and note it on the Inventory sheet.**

Rating the intensity of the stress you are feeling further helps you to tune into your body. In addition, it helps you to objectively measure any changes you experience while using the Process. By having an objective measurement, you are able to receive real-time feed- back on what you are experiencing. This feedback is helpful because when you are dealing with stressful events it is easy for your thinking to become confused. Having a way to receive real-time feedback is helpful in gaining clarity and serenity.

For example, having two sons has presented many stressful situations in my life. By writing down what was triggering my stress, where I felt it and how strong it was, I was able to look at the situation more objectively. Then, when using the Process and experiencing relief, I realized the situation didn't have to make me feel stressed out - I could be concerned without the emotional fallout of being overly stressed. This, in turn, made it easier for me to respond - rather than react - to my children's behavior.

So, give the stress you are feeling a number (don't try to get the number "right", pick the number that feels or seems accurate to you). Then write that number down on the Inventory sheet where it says "Intensity". This is important because I am going to ask you to rate the intensity of the stress you are feeling again, after you have done the Process. This is how you will be able to measure what you are experiencing and receive real-time feedback.

Now you're ready to go through the actual statements in the Pondera Process® for Stress.

# Step 3

**Using the Healthy Heart Hold, go through each of the following statements, keeping your hands in the hold position for 3 deep breaths. Then switch your hands and take 3 more deep breaths, or continue until you feel that you are done with that statement.**

To recap, you started by noticing where you are feeling stress in your body, rating the intensity of the stress on a scale of 0-10 and writing this information down on the Inventory sheet. You also have filled in the blanks in statements 2, 5 & 9 with the terms appropriate to you. Now you are ready to place your hands in the Healthy Heart Hold position and take a few deep breaths to calm and center yourself.

Read the first statement out loud, take 3 deep breaths (fill up your stomach like a balloon), switch your hands and take 3 more deep breaths. Simply repeat this same sequence of expressing the statement out loud and following the same pattern of breathing for all 9 of the statements.

It's that simple!

Here's an additional tip that I don't include in the instructions. Each time you inhale, visualize inhaling golden-white light. I will often use the terms Loving Light or Healing Energy, as well as golden-white light. Visualizing yourself taking in positive energy as you say each statement can enhance the benefits you receive from the Process. You are, in reality, allowing positive energy from your Higher Power to come into your energy system with each statement. I encourage you to visualize what you are expressing, requesting, and allowing.

# Step 4

**Rate the intensity of the stress again. Think about the stress you are clearing and see how it feels in your body now. Rate how intense the stress feels to you now on a scale of 0-10.**

Remember you are rating the intensity in order to provide yourself with real time feedback as you go through the Process.

Having gone through all of the statements, stop and check in with yourself. Think about the item causing you stress and see how it feels to you now. Do you feel it in the same place in your body? Or has it moved to a different area? How strong is the feeling now?

Paying attention to what you feel, where you feel it, and how strong the feeling is, provides you with immediate and valuable feedback.

Use the Inventory sheet to keep track of what you are experiencing as you go through the Pondera Process®.

# Step 5

**Write down any insights on the Inventory sheet.**

It is not uncommon, while using the Pondera Process®, to receive an "aha" or realization of a different way to handle what is causing you stress. Write down any insights you might receive, any thoughts that may come to you about another way to address the event that has been causing you stress. Take note of these insights and give them a try.

# Step 6

**Repeat the Process. If there is still some stress in your body, or any intensity of emotion, return to Step 3 and simply repeat affirmations 2-9, describing what you are feeling in the language that feels right to you now.**

Typically, going through the Pondera Process® once will reduce the stress you are focusing on by approximately 30% to 60%.

Occasionally it will dissipate completely, but you should not be surprised if it doesn't.

The last sentence of this Step says, "…describing what you are feeling in language that feels right to you now." The reason for this is that it is not uncommon for the stress you are feeling over a particular event to move from one spot in your body to a different spot after the first round of the Process. It happens. No worries, just repeat statements 2-9 of Step 3 and fill in the blank in statement 2 with where you feel the stress now. Simply pay attention to what you are feeling and where you are feeling it, changing how you fill in the blanks to reflect where you are now.

## Step 7

**Continue to adapt the language you are using to describe the stress, repeating affirmations 2-9 in Step 3 until all of the discomfort is gone.**

This is just to encourage you not to have a "one and done" mentality toward the Pondera Process® or your well-being.

Also, it is not uncommon for the Pondera Process® to bring to your awareness another related item that is contributing to the stress you are feeling. If that happens, simply focus on the new item, note where you feel the stress in your body and how intense it is, then repeat the Pondera Process® for the new item.

Simply continue to check in with yourself and fill in the blanks of Step 3 with the language that feels right to you in the moment. Stay with the Process, adapting it to meet your needs, until you feel better.

In addition, after going through the Process you may find that what started out as a feeling of stress has become an awareness of other emotions that are causing you distress. For instance, you may initially identify your discomfort as stress, but after going through the Process you realize that you feel angry.

Not a problem. I have adapted the Pondera Process® so that it can help with any emotion you may be feeling. Simply grab a copy of the Pondera Process® for Emotions from my website at www.rebuildingafter.com and use that script for any emotion you are experiencing.

Important: Since I am not a licensed professional and I offer coaching in personal growth, my lawyer insists that I remind you that if you inadvertently experience any distressing reactions while doing the Pondera Process®, then stop and make sure you seek appropriate help. Apart from keeping my lawyer happy, this is a matter of self-care. Use the Process as long as it is helping you. If you have any negative reactions to using the Process, then stop and find someone who can help you.

## Summing up

There you have it. Don't let all the words used to describe the Process fool you into thinking it is complicated. Remember, as a blue-collar spiritual guy, I am always looking to make things as simple and effective as I can. This really is a simple Process to use.

The Process is a great technique for you to have on your journey toward greater serenity and well-being. You can think of it as a staff, or walking stick, which helps you to keep your balance as you are hiking through life.

You can feel confident in using the Process to help reduce your stress and bring more serenity into your life. You don't have to perform the Process perfectly in order to experience positive results. And the more you practice the Pondera Process®, the more likely it is you will get the results you desire.

Now that you have a reliable walking stick to lean on, it would be helpful to have a map which gives you direction, guidance, and confidence as you journey forward. Let's move on to Chapter 8 and look at such a map.

# Resources

As I have taught the Pondera Process® for Stress over the years, many people have approached me and said, "This is great, but I don't want to be opening my eyes in order to read the script. Is there a way for me to keep my eyes closed and be guided through the Process?" In my continuing quest to keep this Process simple, I recorded the Pondera Process® for Stress and you can find it at the link below.

www.rebuildingafter.com/pondera-process-for-stress-audio/

I mentioned in Step 7 above that the Pondera Process® has been adapted to help reduce the intensity of any emotion that is causing you distress. This link will take you to the audio recording which will guide you through the Pondera Process® for Emotions:

www.rebuildingafter.com/pondera-process-for-emotions-audio/

Additionally, I have created a set of videos which further explains the Pondera Process® for Emotions. If you would like a more in-depth description of how to use the Process, plus a demonstration of my using the Process, then this is for you:

www.rebuildingafter.com/pondera-process-for-emotions-video/

## Pondera Process® for Stress

Step 1 Notice what is causing you stress and where you are feeling stress in your body. It is preferable that you write this down on the Inventory sheet.

Step 2 Rate the intensity of the stress on a scale of 0-10 (with 0 being not at all and 10 being the worst it has ever been) and note it on the Inventory sheet.

Step 3 Using the Healthy Heart Hold, go through each of the following statements, keeping your hands in the hold position for 3 deep breaths. Then switch your hands and take 3 more deep breaths, or continue until you feel that you are done with that statement.

1) "I dedicate this session to that which is highest and best for me and anyone else that may benefit from it."

2) "Everything that led up to my feeling stress in my _(body)_ happened, it's over and I am safe now."

3) "I apologize to everyone that I have hurt related to this feeling of stress, including myself. I send us all love, happiness, and peace."

4) "I forgive everyone who hurt me or that I blamed for this feeling of stress, including myself. I send us all love, happiness, and peace."

5) "Thank you, _(Higher Power)_, for healing all of the places in my mind, body, and life where this stress has been stored. Thank you for healing the roots, causes, and deepest origins of this emotion."

6) "All the parts of me that received some benefit from holding on to this stress are healing now."

7) "Whatever is left about this stress is healing now."

8) "I choose to feel peace, serenity and joy where I used to feel stress."

9) "Thank you, _(Higher Power)_, for completely integrating this healing now."

Step 4 Rate the intensity of the stress again. Think about the stress you are clearing and see how it feels in your body now; rate how intense it feels to you now on a scale of zero to ten (0-10). Note the number on the Inventory sheet in the "Intensity" column.

Step 5 Write down any insights on the Inventory sheet.

Step 6 Repeat the Process. If there is still some stress in your body, or any intensity of emotion, return to Step 3 and simply repeat affirmations 2-9, describing what you are feeling in language that feels right to you now.

Step 7 Continue to adapt the language you are using to describe the stress, repeating affirmations 2-9 in Step 3 until all of the discomfort is gone.

Remember, if you inadvertently experience any distressing reactions while doing the Pondera Process, please stop and make sure you seek appropriate help.

## Pondera Process® for Stress

### Instructions for the Pondera Process® for Stress

These instructions will help you to use the Pondera Process in order to reduce the intensity of any stress you are feeling.

<u>Before You Start</u>

- Notice what is causing your stress and where you are feeling any signs of stress in your body. It is preferable that you write this down on the Inventory sheet.

- Rate the intensity of the stress you are feeling on a scale of 0-10 (with 0 being not at all and 10 being the strongest it has ever been) and note it on the Inventory sheet.

- Looking at Step 3 of the Pondera Process for Stress, fill in the blank in statement 2 with the area of your body where you are feeling any signs of stress. Next, decide what you want to insert where I have used the phrase "Higher Power" in statements 5 & 9. You can use God, Universe, Source or any other term that helps you to connect with that Love and Power which is greater than us.

<u>Enjoying the Process</u>

- Place your hands in the Healthy Heart Hold position. Simply place both hands, one hand on top of the other, over your heart.

- Read the first statement on the Pondera Process for Stress, out loud, and take 3 deep breaths. Ideally, breathe in through your nose, filling up your stomach like a balloon. Then slowly exhale through your mouth. Then switch your hands and take 3 more deep breaths.

- Continue through each statement in the Process, taking 3 deep breaths, switching hands and taking 3 more deep breaths, for each of the statements.

- Rate the intensity of the stress again. Think about the stress you are clearing and see how it feels in your body now; rate how intense it feels to you now on a scale of 0-10.

- Write down any insights you receive on the Inventory sheet.

- Repeat the Process. If there is still some stress in your body, or any intensity of emotion, return to Step 3 and repeat statements 2-9, describing what you are feeling in language that feels right to you now.

- Continue to adapt the language you are using to describe the stress, repeating affirmations 2-9 from the Process until you feel that you are done.

Remember, if you inadvertently experience any distressing reactions while doing the Pondera Process, please stop and make sure you seek appropriate help.

## Pondera Process® for Stress

*Rebuilding After...*
Helping People Move Forward With Ease

### Stress Inventory

| Event | Emotions that I feel | Intensity (0 - 10) | Where in my body I feel it | Insight |
|-------|----------------------|--------------------|----------------------------|---------|
|       |                      |                    |                            |         |
|       |                      |                    |                            |         |
|       |                      |                    |                            |         |
|       |                      |                    |                            |         |
|       |                      |                    |                            |         |

# Chapter 8

# The Transformation Process

During the writing of this book I was asked, "Is there a pattern of growth that is common between the different clients you have worked with?" My instinctive response was, "Yes. While everyone is unique in their experience, there are themes and tendencies that are consistent across everyone." Their immediate response was, "Good, you need to include a chapter about the change process."

That is my challenge for this chapter.

Think of the transformation process I am sharing with you as being a map, a map which provides you with an overall picture of what the growth process looks like. While each person's journey will be unique to them in its particulars, there are elements which are common to the growth process. Having the transformation map as a reference point can take away a lot of the uncertainty, hesitation and second-guessing from your progress. Knowing that you are following a well-trodden path is reassuring and comforting.

As with many other parts of this book, I am indebted to the work and writings of many other people. In particular, this chapter draws from the writings of Huston Smith, Michael Beckwith, D.D., Jane Middleton-Moz, M.S., and Lorie L. Dwinell. Their respective writings are noted in the Resources section and I elaborate on Michael Beckwith's thinking in the Appendix.

Let's start to meet the challenge of this chapter by defining what our end goal is. It is always easier to hit a target when you know what you are aiming for. What is it we are trying to accomplish through our self-help activities? The answer depends on whether you are approaching self-help from a 2D or 3D perspective. The traditional 2D answer would be that the goal is to improve some physical or emotional aspect of your life using mind/body techniques. In contrast, I would suggest that a 3D answer is that our goal is to use mind/body/energy techniques to allow the energy of Universal Love to flow into and through us.

Enlightened self-help is taking the steps we need to, in order to live from an identity that we are spirit/energy beings, as well as physical and emotional beings. We can be confident knowing that those steps can lead us to the emotional and physical results we want - along with increasing our experience of peace, serenity, joy, and other desirable side effects. Enlightened self-help is learning to love ourselves as divine, spiritual/energy beings and to pass on that love to everyone and everything around us.

Having a clearer end goal in mind, let me approach the idea of a transformation process by offering a framework which reflects a common pattern of growth that I have seen in myself and my clients. It will help us to take our overall goal of enlightened self-help and break it down into bite-sized pieces.

## 10 Steps toward Transformation

These are the steps I have consistently seen my clients take in their transformational journey. Each person is unique in their journey, but they all follow the general framework of these 10 steps.

1. Become aware that you have a life challenge, be it a problem or a growth point.

2. Acknowledge your losses.

3. Develop a cognitive life raft.

4. Develop an emotional safety net.

5. Accept your coping skills and choose to transform them into thriving skills.

6. Balance out distressing emotions.

7. Balance out limiting beliefs.

8. Reframe old memories through empathy and new understandings.

9. Practice forgiveness and gratitude.

10. Continue to grow in your understanding, healing, and behavior in a way that is highest and best for you. Continue to anchor the identity that you are a spiritual/energy being learning to receive Divine Love and to pass that Love on to everyone and everything around you.

I am indebted to Jane Middleton-Moz and Lorie L. Dwinell for their book, "After the Tears: Helping Adult Children of Alcoholics Heal Their Childhood Trauma" which provided the inspiration for my list. These ten steps, along with an understanding of the Belief Tree discussed in Chapter 6, can help you to determine what will be the next action you take in your own transformational journey.

Let's look at each of the steps in a bit more detail.

**STEP 1:** Become aware. This step asks you to feel and acknowledge the distress you are experiencing, to let go of the denial and avoidance you have used in the past to deaden the emotional pain. If there is a problem in your life causing you distress, then you need to stop denying that there is a problem. Or, on the other hand, you may find life handing you a challenge which creates some anxiety because it would take you out of your comfort zone. Cultivate the inner knowing that you are safe and allow yourself to acknowledge the problem or challenge, even though it feels uncomfortable at first, knowing that the resulting growth you experience will only expand your comfort zone and sense of safety.

In the Resources section of this chapter, I have provided you with a link to the Pondera Process® for Loving Light. This is an easy and effective way to develop a connection with your Higher Power and to allow the presence of divine love to support you emotionally.

**STEP 2:** Acknowledge your losses. This step is about letting go of self-judgement for having a particular problem in your life. The anger and ODSR which were such a problem for me came out of my coping with my childhood environment. In order to move forward, I had to acknowledge that they had served me in that environment but did not serve me well later in life. To move forward it is necessary to have compassion and understanding that you did the best you could with the cards you were dealt. It is realizing that you are not crazy, rather, that you are having a normal reaction to an abnormal and painful life.

**STEP 3:** Develop a cognitive life raft. In order to move forward in your journey, it is essential that you become intentional about developing an intellectual understanding of the problem or challenge in front of you. This increased understanding of the dynamics behind your challenge helps to further validate your losses and glimpse a path forward. When you increase your understanding of the challenge in front of you, it is easier to feel emotionally safe to continue moving toward a solution. As Middleton-Moz and Dwinell describe it, "The cognitive life raft becomes an intellectual guide - an understanding of the beginning, middle, and end of the process of healing wounds of the past".

Developing this understanding of your problem or challenge doesn't mean reading just one more book or watching one more video. It means gaining a sufficient understanding of your situation to realize you are not alone, that you are not crazy, that other people have gone through similar problems and challenges, that there is hope. When that light bulb comes on for you, take a step toward bringing more light into your life.

**STEP 4:** Develop an emotional safety net. As I have mentioned elsewhere in this book, you will not make progress if you do not feel safe moving forward. It is imperative that you intentionally create a safe and supportive environment from which you can grow. This can be a specific counselor, a support group, a sponsor, or any other resource that helps you to feel safe moving forward. The Pondera Process® for Loving Light can also help you to develop a personal emotional safety net.

**STEP 5:** Accept your coping skills and choose to transform them into thriving skills. It takes a tremendous amount of energy and determination to continue coping with a distressing or dysfunctional life situation. It is valuable and important that you realize that you have already demonstrated the necessary strength and determination you will need in order to make positive changes in your life. All that is required is to make a decision, a choice, to put that same energy and determination into growing toward greater serenity rather than choosing just to cope with an unhealthy situation. You are never stuck - any life situation can be improved to some degree.

You have already shown that you have a capacity to thrive. Anybody who can survive can also thrive.

**STEP 6:** Balance out distressing emotions as you become aware of them. Referring back to the Belief Tree illustration (Chapter 6), it is easiest to start with the leaves and work your way down to the roots of a problem or challenge. While you can go straight to an underlying memory, the process for most occasions is like peeling an onion - we start with the outer layers and peel away to the core.

I say "balance out distressing emotions" because that has been the most effective approach I have found. By understanding that emotions are a form of energy and that the distressing emotion is disrupted energy, you can be intentional about balancing the energy through the Pondera Process® or another energy balancing technique. By balancing the energy of the emotion, you create greater serenity and clarity for yourself, which in turn opens you up to inspiration and insight into any underlying beliefs or memories which would benefit from some loving attention.

**STEP 7:** Balance out limiting beliefs. After balancing the energy around any emotions which are causing you distress, you then want to balance the energy around any limiting beliefs which you sense are contributing to the problem or challenge on which you are focused. Using the Pondera Process® for Beliefs is an effective way to unhook from the energy of old beliefs and to create a space for you to shift toward a more empowering belief.

**STEP 8:** Balance out old memories and reframe them through empathy and new understandings. As I talked about it in Chapter 6, memories are your interpretation of a past event. When you use the Pondera Process® for Memories, you are again able to unhook from the energy of an old memory and reinterpret it from your current vantage point.

For example, I had many memories around my dad's drinking that fueled my anger and I was not able to change the way I saw those scenes from my past because of the intense emotion connected to those memories. There were three elements which empowered me to reinterpret those past events and thus reduce the need I felt to become angry.

First, I had to balance out the energy around the old memory and be open to learning a new understanding of what I experienced. Without balancing the energy around the memory first, there was too much internal resistance for me to view the scene differently.

Second, as I took the emotional charge out of the old memory, I was able to realize that my dad was the product of his own upbringing. He had lost his mother while quite young and many of his family members drank as a way to cope with life's challenges.

Third, the increased understanding that I was not bound to my childhood interpretation of old events, the increased understanding of why my father drank the way he did and the greater empathy for him made it possible for me to reinterpret those scenes from my life from a less fearful and a healthier point of view.

This step is especially important for all of us who blame ourselves for the destructive behavior of our family members. It is very difficult to let go of any feelings of shame or guilt until you are able to see the past through wiser, healthier, and more compassionate eyes.

**STEP 9:** Practice gratitude and forgiveness. Entire books have been written on each of these topics, and rightly so. I have found that forgiveness and gratitude, correctly understood, are the keystones in moving toward the desired endpoint of any transformative journey. They are critical to your being able to live from the identity of a spiritual being and allowing Love to flow into and through you.

As the Roman philosopher Cicero is often quoted as saying, "Gratitude is not only the greatest of virtues, but the parent of all the others." From an energy point of view, when you practice gratitude, you have to first allow into your life the positive energy of that for which you are grateful. The active practice of gratitude is a surefire way for you to allow Divine Love to flow into you.

Forgiveness is one way we allow that Divine Love to flow through us and out to others. Now, there are a whole lot of misunderstandings about forgiveness because contemporary writers have tried to explain it from a 2D perspective. Forgiveness is a 3D phenomenon and can be best understood from a 3D perspective. I will save a more extensive discussion of this point for another book. For now, I will merely point out that you will benefit significantly when you understand that forgiveness is not an act of will power from yourself (a 2D understanding) but is an allowing of forgiveness to flow from Source and out through you.

Gratitude and forgiveness. These are essential for you to continue to grow through the multitude of life's challenges that you will face in your lifetime.

**STEP 10:** Continue to grow in your identity as a spiritual/energy being, allowing Divine Love to flow into and through you.

This brings us back to the endpoint I identified at the beginning of this chapter. The purpose of enlightened self-help is for us to learn how to live from this expanded understanding of who we are and why we are here, to allow the energy of Universal Love to flow into and through us. Learning to live from a 3D perspective, and it is a learned ability, is the most certain way to reduce the level of stress in your life and to enjoy greater serenity during your journey on earth.

Looking at your growth journey with the aid of this ten-step transformation process can help you to find greater hope and joy in "The Game of Life and How to Play it", as Florence Scovel Shinn aptly titled her classic book. Learn to play life from a 3D perspective and the ride will be much more fun and enjoyable.

As you come to the end of this chapter, you may be thinking, "That's great, Larry. You have shared with us these ideas for a transformation process, but I thought you were a blue-collar spiritual guy. How do we make this even more practical? What practical steps can I take to continue down a path of enlightened self-help?"

Good question. Let's move on to the last chapter and see what some productive next steps can be for your journey.

## Resources

Pondera Process for Loving Light www.rebuildingafter.com/pondera-process-for-loving-light-audio/

Pondera Process for Gratitude www.rebuildingafter.com/pondera-process-for-gratitude-audio/

Michael Bernard Beckwith, *Life Visioning: A Transformative Process for Activating Your Unique Gifts and Highest Potential,* (Boulder, CO.: Sounds True, 2012)

Daniel Goleman, *Emotional Intelligence: Why it can Matter More Than IQ,* (New York: Bantam, 2005)

Jane Middleton-Moz, M.S. and Lorie L. Dwinell, *After the Tears: Helping Adult Children of Alcoholics Heal Their Childhood Trauma,* (Deerfield Beach, FL.: Health Communications, 2010)

Florence Scovel Shinn, *The Game of Life and How to Play It,* (New York: Simon & Schuster, 2001)

# Chapter 9

# Next Steps

We have come to the final chapter of our journey, moving from a traditional self-help approach to life's problems and challenges toward an enlightened self-help approach. What do you do now?

I think the best way for me to answer this important question is to take you through the sequence of questions I would lead a typical client through over a series of sessions. Naturally, not every person moves forward at the same pace. It's just like hiking up a path toward a beautiful vista, different people will move at different speeds, and some will want to pause more frequently than others.

In addition, I will share with you what some of the common issues and sticking points are as a person moves forward in their journey. Of course, no two people are the same and every situation has its own unique twists, but there are elements which are common to most issues. Having a heads up about these common elements will help you to know that you are not alone when you encounter them and help you to move forward with greater ease.

Let's get started, knowing that you can move back and forth through my observations and recommendations in a way that will be highest and best for you.

When I work with someone, I start by providing them with a context for what we will be doing together (basically a 10 minute summary of this book) and what they can expect from our work together. I remind them that our goal is to bring greater peace, joy, and serenity into their life, not to stir up old pain and suffering. I stress that we will move forward at a pace that feels safe to them at all times, that they will not allow themselves to grow through a problem or challenge unless they feel safe doing so. Then I use the metaphor of an onion to explain how we will gradually peel back the layers of whatever is causing them distress until we get to the core of an issue and transform that core into something that will serve what is highest and best for them now.

Having created a safe environment and an expectation that we are looking to create greater serenity, I ask the client, "If you had a magic wand and could change any one aspect of your life today, what would you choose? What are you willing to let go of so that you can feel better?"

Ask yourself the same questions and note the first thing(s) that come to your mind. That is where you start your journey. That is the point of least resistance for you, where you feel the safest making a change. This is an ideal place for you to experience how the Pondera Process® or another energy technique can effectively help you right now.

The magic wand question is a simple and safe way for you to identify an issue where you can experience the power of a 3D self-help technique.

An alternative for those who are skittish about using the Pondera Process® on an aspect of their life, and some clients have been hesitant, I encourage them to use the Pondera Process® for Loving Light. This is a recording I created for folks who feel cut off from anything greater than themselves and, thus, have trouble trusting that an energy technique can help them. The Pondera Process® for Loving Light helps the person to allow in some positive energy and to feel the benefit of doing so. This, in turn, gives them the assurance and confidence to use the Process on the item they identified with their magic wand.

So, you have identified a particular item which is causing you distress and you have used the Pondera Process® for Loving Light to begin feeling better, but you also feel some resistance, some hesitation, about using the Process on the next layer of your onion. What might be causing your hesitation about feeling better?

One of my early teachers, Mary Sise, writes in the book *The Energy of Belief: Psychology's Power Tools to Focus Intention and Release Blocking Beliefs* about four beliefs which she called primary blocking beliefs, beliefs that will prevent you from moving forward on a path of growth and healing. She identifies those beliefs as safety, deservedness, relationships, and the future. Let's touch on each of these briefly, as they can stop your growth journey very quickly.

**Safety.** Feeling safe is a primal instinct, it is essential for survival. While we can easily grasp this truth for our physical safety, we are often slow to realize it is also true for our emotional wellbeing. If you feel vulnerable, if you feel unsure that taking the next step of growth for you is safe for you or someone you care about, then you will hesitate and hold back.

**Deservedness.** If you have feelings of shame or unworthiness about yourself, then you will say that you want to feel better but always find a reason not to move toward greater serenity. Also, it is not uncommon for someone to hold on to a problem because they carry a lot of guilt and believe they need to be punished.

**Relationships.** What will be the impact of your getting better be on your current relationships? Are you fearful of "rocking the boat" in any of your important relationships? It's good to intentionally ask yourself this question because as you grow you will inevitably attract and feel more comfortable with a new mix of friends, friends who support the happier you.

**Future.** This is the belief that your problems are permanent. You have had them for so long that you don't have a lot of hope that your life can be made better.

I was tempted to let my own healing and growth be stopped by this one when it came to making progress on my anger issues. There were two things which propelled me to move forward. One, I was sufficiently sick and tired of the emotional pain from staying the same that I was willing to try again for greater peace and serenity. Second, this time I was using a 3D solution. All my other attempts to change had used a 2D approach and resulted in frustration. Using the 3D approach gave me enough renewed hope to move forward.

If part of you wants to make a change and let go of something which has caused your ongoing distress, yet another part of you wants to stay the same, ask yourself if one of the above feels true to you. Your hesitation is probably unconscious and it is in asking yourself good questions that you can bring your concerns to your conscious awareness in order to address them.

Before moving on, I will share two more valuable questions to ask yourself. I learned these from Carol Look, another teacher and practitioner that I benefitted from early on. Ask yourself, "What is the upside of holding on to this problem?" Then ask yourself, "What is the downside of letting this problem go?" The reality is that if you are receiving some benefit from having a problem, you are not going to let it go unless you have an idea of how you will replace the old benefit.

When I am working with a client and I sense some hesitation on their part, I immediately go to these six items (safety, deservedness, relationships, future, upside, and downside) to see if they can shed some light on what the person is feeling but has not been able to express.

So, what do you do if you feel stuck early on? I always start folks off with the Pondera Process® for Loving Light and ask them to use it on a daily basis. It has been reliable in helping folks to feel a sense of security and renewed hope so that they can take one more, small step toward greater peace, serenity, clarity, and joy. In addition, I might introduce them to the Pondera Process® for Emotions and/or Beliefs in order to get them unstuck.

Having identified the first issue a client wants to move through, I check to see if they are beating themselves up for even having this problem. As I mentioned in Step 2 of the 10 Steps toward Transformation list, it is necessary to let go of self-judgment for having any particular problem in your life. To accomplish this, I help the client use the Pondera Process® for Beliefs or Emotions in order to reframe the way they look at the problem. Most often, the problem started out as a coping strategy which served them early on but is now causing them distress. Once the understanding is brought to the client's awareness, it is easier for them to let go of their attachment to the problem and move toward a solution which is highest and best for them.

Sometimes it is difficult to let go of self-judgment when working on your own. If that happens to you, I encourage you to reach out to a support group or another individual to assist you. We are designed to live and grow as part of a community. Don't isolate yourself and insist on doing all of your growth work on your own.

Support groups are also valuable in helping you to move through Steps 3 & 4 of the 10 Step Process toward Transformation. It is highly unlikely that any problem or challenge that is causing you distress is yours and yours alone. Indeed, there is nothing new under the sun and you are smart to benefit from the experience and study of other people who can support you - and your journey will be much smoother.

Early on in working with a client, I help them to appreciate how emotionally strong they have been while coping with, and oftentimes enduring, a distressing problem in their life. Now, in order to grow through a problem, they (and you) need to transfer that emotional energy into actions which lead to greater serenity, actions which lead to thriving and not just surviving.

The reason a client (and you) feel stuck is that the energy surrounding the problem is stuck in your personal energy system. By using the Pondera Process® you can free up that stuck energy, you take your foot off of the brake, which makes it easier for you to move forward.

The important takeaway is that you already have shown the capacity necessary for growing toward greater serenity. It's simply a matter of redirecting your emotional strength away from coping and toward growing.

The first 5 steps of the 10 Steps toward Transformation list set a foundation which my clients (and you) can build from. Think of them as the tools necessary to help you peel back the onion that is your problem. You can skip to Step 6 and start using the Pondera Process® appropriate to your needs, but if you don't get the results you want, then take a step back and see if you would be well served to shore up your foundation for growth.

When you have a solid foundation in place, then Steps 6 – 8 are a piece of cake. As you identify emotions, beliefs, or memories which cause you distress, which no longer contribute to your wellbeing, simply use the appropriate Process to shift that item. Remember, everything is a form of energy, and when you shift the energy around an item, you shift the item itself.

When I'm working with a client, the sessions become an ongoing conversation where I help them to articulate their distress. I then lead them through the relevant Process, which helps them to unhook from the energy which is keeping them stuck. Then I guide them to replace or reframe the old emotion, belief, or memory in a way that serves their wellbeing now. The consistent result is an experience of increased peace, serenity, and insight which empowers them to take the next step in their journey toward what is highest and best for them.

This is a pattern of awareness, intention, insight, and action which my clients can always do on their own. In fact, I am constantly encouraging them to use the Process on their own for two primary reasons. First, I want them to keep moving forward at as fast a pace as they feel comfortable with. Second, I don't want them to become dependent on me, thinking that the Pondera Process® only works when I do it with them. I am just a guide and a coach; it is their intention and direct connection to a Source of loving energy that makes the difference.

Just like my many clients, you can also use the Process to help yourself gain greater serenity and insight. In those situations where you prefer to have someone alongside you, reach out to a supportive friend or energy psychology practitioner to help you. The point is, you are not dependent on another person for you to begin feeling better today.

When you use a 3D approach like the Pondera Process®, you do discover new hope for self-help.

Next, on your journey toward wellbeing, actively practice gratitude and forgiveness on a frequent basis. These are consistent practices which continue to power you forward. They are two practices which I am consistently educating and reminding my clients about.

Let me share a couple of thoughts on gratitude and forgiveness which can help support you.

As I mentioned earlier, the active practice of gratitude is a sure-fire way for you to allow Divine Love to flow into you. Let me share a practical way for you to easily practice gratitude.

I regularly ask my clients to share with me something that puts a smile on their face, something that provides them with some sense of increased peace, joy, or hope. I then ask them to place both of their hands over their heart and to breathe deeply while visualizing in as great of detail as they can, that object or memory which they have chosen. I ask them to visualize it in enough detail that they can feel the positive energy of that image in their body.

Visualizing something you are grateful for has a documented positive effect on your brain and your nervous system, and throughout your body. Plus, it feels good!

So, here's what I encourage you to do. Make a list of memories or objects which bring a smile to your face; that contribute to an increased sense of peace, joy, or hope in you. These can be memories of experiences that you have had, places you have been, something in nature that you resonate with, perhaps a beloved pet, a person you have known, or anything which inspires the high vibration feelings of peace, joy, or hope in you. Write down this list so that you can refer to it whenever you choose. In this way, you are creating a library of images which you can draw from; images which you can actively visualize and feel positive effects of, just like you did the first time.

By intentionally and actively practicing gratitude with this type of visualization, you become increasingly comfortable with allowing yourself to receive and experience the feeling of positive energy. You begin to trust that this can happen for you and to feel safe in letting it happen. This inevitably leads to your wanting to feel even more peace, joy, and serenity which motivates you to continue on your journey to greater well-being.

Because this is such a powerful practice, I created the Pondera Process® for Gratitude which helps you to visualize and experience the benefits from your library of images. It takes less than ten minutes to do. Use this or another technique to practice gratitude on a regular basis and feel the quality of your life improve. You will be grateful that you are practicing gratitude.

As for forgiveness, one of the main understandings that I impart to my clients is that they have been taught to think of forgiveness as an all-or-nothing proposition; that when you forgive somebody you have to forgive them completely. In reality, most of the time we didn't feel safe completely forgiving someone or something. The result is that any effort toward forgiveness leads to frustration, and our choosing to hold onto the hurt instead of being frustrated by trying to let it go.

This is a 2D understanding of forgiveness and it focuses on willpower to make it happen. Instead, think of forgiveness as a seed that you can plant in your heart and then water it. Allow forgiveness to grow in you at a rate that feels safe to you. By taking a growth (3D) approach instead of an all-or-nothing (2D) approach, you give yourself space to take on new understandings and to find other ways of protecting yourself.

Remember, forgiveness is how you let go of old hurts which continue to cause you distress. It is how you stop letting a person or an experience have control over your wellbeing. Forgiveness is something that flows through you, not something that comes from you.

All of this brings us back to the importance of practicing gratitude. The more you are intentional in allowing positive energy to flow into you, the more you become comfortable with this dynamic, the easier it will be to trust the Love behind the positive energy and feel safe letting go of old hurts.

This, once again, brings us back to the endpoint of the transformation process which I shared with you at the beginning of Chapter 8. As you use the suggestions in this chapter to build into your life, the tools and techniques I have discovered during my journey, you will increasingly live a 3D life and experience the benefits of expressing your identity as a spiritual/energy being.

Let me share one more observation before we end our journey together. The path we are on does not go in a straight line. That probably doesn't surprise you, but it is common for my clients to feel frustrated when they don't experience steady forward progress.

Think of it this way. As humans, we are designed to grow, just as all living things in nature are designed to grow. And just as with your favorite plant, there are seasons to your growth. You and I were built to grow in an unfolding, cyclical, stair-step pattern (pick the metaphor you prefer) not in a straight line.

Remember when I talked about needing to feel safe before you will allow yourself to grow? It does not feel emotionally safe to continuously grow. We all need new opportunities to pause, to integrate the new insights and understandings we are gaining.

We all need opportunities to process the new-found positive energy coming into our life.

In addition, the path is not straight because part of living a 3D life entails letting go of the need to control the direction you are going, letting go of the belief that you can control life and always keep it going in a straight line. Instead, you become increasingly comfortable in trusting a Source of loving energy at the heart of the universe and allow the serendipities of life, the unexpected twists and turns, which bring you experiences of joy and serenity that you would never experience if you traveled in a straight line.

Bottom line, the twists and turns of your journey are normal and to be expected. The plateaus of growth you experience are opportunities for you to catch your breath, to enjoy longer and deeper insights and understandings of the journey you are on, and to enjoy the new vistas before you.

Based on my experience, and the experience of my many clients, I can tell you this. Peace, serenity, clarity, joy and greater wellbeing are yours for the asking. All you need to do is learn to ask from a 3D view of life.

May my journey toward a more empowering understanding of self-help and renewed hope be an inspiration and a guide for your own journey.

Enjoy the experience!

# Resources

For tools and tips to support your journey, go to www.rebuildingafter. com and join my mailing list, if you have not done so already. This is a great way to receive ongoing encouragement.

Check out the resources in the Store at rebuildingafter.com. There is a variety of audios and videos, all designed to support your growth and understanding.

Most importantly, journey on!

Continue on a path that enables you to tap into the power within you and within the Universe. Continue on the path toward acquiring a more empowered form of self-help and reap the benefits of increased serenity, joy, peace, and all things positive!

# *Appendix*

# Energy Intelligence and More

Originally, the content in this Appendix was included in Chapter 8. But then it became clear this was TMI (Too Much Information) for that chapter and how the book was flowing.

At the same time, I felt strongly that this was important content and needed a wider audience. Hence, I am offering it here, in the Appendix.

I introduced the concept of energy intelligence (EnQ) earlier, in Chapter 5. Now I want to expand on the concept and hopefully spark a larger dialogue. Regardless, it is in the best interest of each of us to increasingly grow in our understanding of ourselves as having an energetic dimension as well as physical and mental dimensions. Hopefully, the five aspects of EnQ which I'll share will make it easier for you to see how you can grow your own energy intelligence and reap the benefits of your growth.

In addition, we will once again look at the transformation process, only from a higher point of view. We will look at one portion of the writings from Michael Beckwith in his book *Life Visioning: A Transformative Process for Activating Your Unique Gifts and Highest Potential*. In it, Beckwith presents a four-stage process which illustrates the changing perspectives we go through as we grow. His model is a bit more conceptual than my 10 Step

Transformation Process, but the ideas and understandings he shares are quite valuable and are a necessary part of any spiritual/emotional growth.

Having said all that, let me share with you what didn't fit into Chapter 8 but needed to be part of this book.

## Emotional Intelligence (EQ) and Energy Intelligence (EnQ)

In 1995, Daniel Goleman released a book entitled *Emotional Intelligence: Why It Can Matter More Than IQ*. More than five million copies have been sold worldwide since its release and the book has redefined how we define "intelligence" and has significantly impacted the field of personal development/self-help.

Goleman, who was a science writer at *The New York Times*, uses the term "emotional intelligence" to bring together a wide range of scientific findings from several related fields of research.

Prior to 1995, intelligence had typically been defined as a person's intellectual/mental capacity. Goleman's writing challenged that assumption and showed that many people who were not considered "smart", were intelligent in emotional terms and became highly successful people. He showed that the traditional intelligence measurement was true but incomplete. People also have an emotional IQ, and their emotional IQ can be raised through training and learning, just like their intellectual/mental capacity can be raised.

I would suggest that we are now at a similar place to where we were in1995. We can now bring together a wide range of scientific findings from related fields of research which support the understanding that we have an energy dimension to ourselves, just as we have an emotional dimension, and that our energy IQ can also be raised through training and learning.

Just as Goleman showed that the traditional measurement of intelligence was a valid but incomplete measurement of a person's overall intelligence, so we can now show that both traditional and emotional IQ are valid, but are still an incomplete measurement of a person's overall intelligence. It is time to include energy intelligence into the mix. Becoming intelligent in all three aspects of our full nature as humans is just a smart way to live.

We will all benefit as an increasing number of people become purposeful in developing their mental, emotional, and energy intelligences.

So, let's take a closer look at how Goleman explained emotional intelligence and see how his model can help us to explain and understand energy intelligence.

## Emotional Intelligence (EQ)

Goleman identified five elements which make up a person's emotional intelligence:

1. **Self-awareness.** Goleman describes this as "knowing one's emotions". It is the ability to recognize a feeling as it happens and is considered by Goleman as being the keystone of emotional intelligence.

2. **Managing emotions.** Learning the skill of "handling feelings so they are appropriate". It is the ability to express emotions in a manner proportionate to the circumstance. The goal is to maintain emotional balance, not to suppress your feelings or to express them unchecked. Goleman also stresses the importance of self-soothing, the ability to comfort yourself when you are upset, as a fundamental life skill.

3. **Motivating yourself.** The skill of "marshalling emotions in the service of a goal" is a trait Goleman identifies as being present in all high performers. He goes on to identify some of the key indicators of this as being:
   - the ability to delay gratification

- a general sense of enthusiasm
- a feeling of confidence and resourcefulness
- being flexible enough to find an alternative solution
- a persistent sense of hope
- an underlying sense of optimism: having a strong expectation that everything will turn out all right

4. **Recognizing emotions in others.** This is empathy, the "ability to know how another feels". Goleman refers to this as "the fundamental people skill". He goes on to stress that the more open we are to understanding our own emotions, the more skilled we will be in reading and understanding other people's feelings.

5. **Handling relationships.** This is having "skill in managing emotions in others", of having "social competence".

## Energy Intelligence (EnQ)

In Chapter 5, I described energy intelligence as the ability to understand your body's energy system, to identify disruptions in your energy system and to restore balance, harmony, and flow to your energy system. Accordingly, I would identify the following five elements as components of energy intelligence.

1. **Energy awareness.** This is knowing that you have a subtle energy system and noticing when you feel a disruption in your energy system. It is knowing that any distressing emotion which you feel is the physical expression of a disruption in your subtle energy system.

2. **Energy management.** Learning to care for your energy system and to bring it back into balance when you experience a disruption. It is choosing to use energy techniques to

manage the intensity and impact of emotion on your thinking and well-being, enabling you to express your emotions in a manner proportionate to the circumstance. It is also learning to protect yourself from the negative energy of other people and/or toxic situations.

3. **Intention.** This is the conscious choice to tap into a Source of energy greater than ourselves, to receive and allow to flow through us an eternal and universal energy of Love. It is looking past your emotional self and choosing to be in alignment with a loving energy which underlies everything. When we exercise intention and address the needs of our subtle energy system, it is much easier to cultivate the emotions and beliefs which Goleman identifies as qualities of motivating yourself.

4. **Gratitude.** Engaging in an active practice of gratitude which requires you to acknowledge and allow into your personal energy system the positive energy of any particular experience. Gratitude has repeatedly been found to be one of the most powerful practices for improving your energetic, and thus your emotional, well-being.

5. **Forgiveness.** Learning to allow the positive energy of forgiveness to flow through you and out to another person, group, or situation. Gaining a healthy understanding of what forgiveness is, and what it is not, helps you to detach from the negative energy of past experiences and to feel safe in the present.

The last two elements are what I consider to be cornerstones of cultivating and maintaining a healthy energy system. While there are many other skills and techniques that can significantly contribute to our energetic well-being, I have found gratitude and forgiveness to be the cornerstones. Entire books can and have been written on each of these topics, but for our purposes it is sufficient to simply note that gratitude and forgiveness are fundamental elements of energy intelligence.

## An illustration, please

In his discussion on emotional intelligence, Goleman spends several pages talking about anger and rage. He uses the basic emotion of anger to show how rational thought can be hijacked when anger is triggered and not appropriately managed.

Let me illustrate how energy intelligence complements emotional intelligence by recounting my journey in dealing with the significant anger issues I wrestled with for over fifty years, an emotional challenge I was able to grow through only with a combination of emotional intelligence *and* energy intelligence.

As I mentioned in the introduction, my dad struggled with his own emotional pain and used alcohol to cope from before I was born. As a child of an alcoholic, the emotional climate in our house felt uncertain to me and I was conditioned to be on high alert from an early age. My life experience was just like Goleman describes in his book *Emotional Intelligence*. There were more occasions than I can count when I was emotionally hijacked and reacted to events in my life in a less than constructive manner.

It was the pain of those repeated reactions and the inadequacy of a traditional 2D psychological approach to produce results that motivated me to look for a better answer.

Only when I combined what I had learned about emotional intelligence with what I learned about working with my energy system, when I learned energy intelligence, was I able to respond rather than react to events which would have provoked my anger in the past.

It was from my experience, the experience of my many clients, and all the studying I have done, that the five elements of EnQ began to emerge.

My exposure to NLP introduced me to the concept of energy being an underlying dynamic of emotions, beliefs, and memories. I developed energetic awareness.

Having become aware, and being motivated to minimize my anger issues, I actively learned energy psychology techniques which equipped me to experience energy management. When I recognized that my energy was being disrupted by noticing the distress I felt, I was able to intentionally help myself energetically and as a result, help myself emotionally.

This journey, which I have been on for fifteen years, led to what is in this book and to my realizing the importance of intention. Relying on myself, which a 2D approach to self-help calls for, was inadequate and incomplete. When I embraced a 3D approach to self-help and utilized intention, I was able to access a source of loving energy greater than myself which made all the difference in the results I experienced. It was the utilization of intention inherent to the energy techniques I learned, which made the primary difference in my being able to stop having a hair trigger temper and to turn down the intensity of my anger.

Now, I would have limited energy intelligence to just these three elements. But my experience and an abundance of spiritual literature, all saying the same thing in different ways, pointed to the importance of including gratitude and forgiveness as important elements of EnQ.

Gratitude is a powerful way of cultivating your awareness and acceptance of loving energy into your life. Gratitude fuels the batteries which power your intention to exercise intention. The active practice of gratitude helps me to see past the distress all around me and to focus on the positive which is intrinsic to the energy underlying everything. Distress is an aberration of the intended and normal state of energy, gratitude reminds us of that truth and helps us to stay centered in that truth.

The more I learned different ways to practice and feel gratitude, the easier it became for me to bring intention to all aspects of my life.

Forgiveness, in turn, is the active expression of intention and is a fundamental way for us to balance the disrupted energy around any emotion, belief, or memory which causes us distress. Because of the previous four elements in EnQ above, I have been able to practice forgiveness and to detach from a variety of life experiences which had conditioned me to have a quick and intense anger. By practicing forgiveness toward people, events, and myself for those experiences which made me feel unsafe and contributed to my short fuse, I have been able to bring my temper and anger back into balance, I am better able to express my anger in a manner more appropriate to my circumstance.

The net result is that I am now much more likely to respond, instead of react, to circumstances which would have provoked my hair trigger anger in the past. And the net result of that healing and growth is a great deal more serenity, peace, joy, and hope in my life.

A reward well worth the effort and the journey.

As you can see, just as the 2D paradigm is correct but incomplete, emotional intelligence is also correct but incomplete. When you allow yourself to move toward a 3D paradigm and cultivate energy intelligence, you can replace frustration with results and all the benefits that come from personal growth. EnQ will enhance your EQ and empower you toward even greater results and benefits.

While the concept of energy intelligence can make a significant contribution to the quality of your life, it is equally important to try and make these ideas and concepts as practical as possible. To that end, let me next share with you one part of the writing from Michael Beckwith's book *Life Visioning: A Transformative Process for Activating Your Unique Gifts and Highest Potential.*

## The Four Stages of Evolutionary GroWth

Rev. Michael Beckwith is the founder and spiritual director of the Agape International Spiritual Center. He has been a noted and acclaimed teacher on a practical approach to spirituality and the science of inner transformation for over three decades. In his book, *Life Visioning*, Beckwith identifies four stages which every person must move through in order to reach an end goal of living from their identity as a spiritual being. To quote Beckwith, "The four stages were created as a means of offering a template of the evolution of consciousness, as well as describing the mindsets and behavioral patterns that must be cultivated and released in order to progress from stage to stage."

Let's take a look at Beckwith's four stage transformation model.

Beckwith refers to **Stage One** as victim consciousness. At this level of spiritual evolution, the dominant mindset is "life is being done to me by *it*". "It" can be anything outside of the person which they believe controls their destiny. This can be their DNA, their parents, how they look, how smart other people say they are, having a medical condition, or anything else which they believe controls the quality of their life and "makes" them a victim. Victims believe they are powerless.

People at this level tend to lack self-awareness and are looking for someone or something to blame for the poor quality of their life. They tend to react to life rather than respond to life's challenges. More often than not, they are looking for something or someone to make them feel happy rather than understanding that happiness comes from within.

A key challenge for a Stage One person is give up blame and to learn that they are responsible for their own happiness. In Stage One, it is about learning that you can tap into a Power greater than yourself and begin to be proactive rather than reactive to the twists and turns of life.

I felt like a victim and powerless in my struggles with anger and having an ODSR (overdeveloped sense of responsibility). It was always someone or something else that made me angry, I was never getting angry by choice. I relied on willpower to try and change my behavior. The result was a lot of frustration, self-judgement, and very little progress.

Beckwith goes on to describe **Stage Two** as Manifester Consciousness. This is where the person believes "...that things happen 'to it by me'. Their mind-set is empowered by an 'I make it happen' application of the law of manifestation". In this stage, the individual is beginning to realize that they are a creator in the quality of their life and begin to employ the use of intention, visualization, affirmations, etc., in bringing about improvements to their life.

While this Stage is an improvement over seeing yourself as a victim, it still maintains a limited focus by putting the emphasis on self. This Stage tends to be focused on acquisition and accomplishment, on exerting control over your life experience.

In order to continue evolving and growing past this Stage, it is necessary to release the need to control your life. The challenge is to realize and embrace the larger reality that you are safe even when you cannot direct every facet of your life. As Beckwith puts it, growing through this Stage means, "There is a growing sense of Oneness with Source and how it corresponds to its own nature within us. In other words, when we focus on its (Source) qualities of unconditional love, compassion, generosity, joy, bliss, peace, it corresponds to these same qualities which are inherently within each of us".

Later in the chapter he notes, "One must step out of ego self-absorption and relate to giving as well as receiving, to sharing successes with others", that "In moving beyond Stage Two, it is vital to understand the necessity of surrender" and that "To surrender is to yield to the next stage of your evolution". It is saying, "I'm available to what wants to evolve and emerge through me and I'm willing to practice and embody what it takes for it to do so".

**Stage Three** in Beckwith's evolution paradigm is Channel Consciousness. This stage is where "you become a clear, pure channel" and allow Source, your Higher Power and its qualities, to flow through you. This is a state of being where you allow love, compassion, forgiveness, etc., to flow through you - rather than your trying through willpower to be loving, compassionate, forgiving, etc.

Flow is a good word to describe your state of being when you are experiencing Stage Three. Another way to describe it is "being in the zone". It is the experience you have when your intention is clear and heart centered; when you relax and allow the Universe to unfold its purpose through you; when you no longer try to make something happen and allow what is highest and best for all to come forth.

Beckwith summarizes this Stage well when he says, "This is the crux of what it means to be a spiritual being having a human incarnation: to discover, accept, and express our inheritance of oneness with Source and channel its essence of excellence as we deliver our gifts, talents, and skills in the world. We cannot accomplish this simply by willing it to be so. Only by surrendering the ego's false sense of control and engaging in spiritual practice can we open ourselves to the full expression of Channel Consciousness".

**Stage Four** in Beckwith's model is called Being Consciousness. Whereas in Stage One we see ourselves as a victim; in Stage Two we see ourselves as controlling events in our life through our mind; in Stage Three we see ourselves as being a channel with Source flowing through us to create our life. In Stage Four there is no longer a sense of separation between ourselves and our Higher Power. To quote Beckwith, "For those living in Being Consciousness, there no longer remains a dividing line between oneself and Source. The living fire of Oneness has consumed any residue of separation."

Clearly, as long as we have a body there will be a degree of separation between ourselves and Source. However, while we have a physical separation, we can still experience the feeling of being connected and one with Source. We can still experience the inward certainty that there is more to life than meets the eye and that we are connected to it. Stage Four is where we begin to sense and feel our identity as a spiritual being connected to something greater than ourselves, where we become comfortable with and increasingly embrace our identity as a spiritual/energy being.

This state of being is described well by Jill Bolte Taylor, Ph.D., in her book *My Stroke of Insight*: *A Brain Scientist's Personal Journey*. A Harvard trained brain scientist, in 1996 she experienced a massive stroke which shut down the left side of her brain, the cognitive and rational part of the brain. What is unique about her story is that she was able to observe and document not only the event but her recovery process with the trained insight and expertise of a brain scientist. She describes one consequence of the left side of her brain shutting down this way, "As the language centers in my left hemisphere grew increasingly silent and I became detached from the memories of my life, I was comforted by an expanding sense of grace. In this void of higher cognition and details pertaining to my normal life, my consciousness soared into an all-knowingness, a 'being at one' with the universe, if you will. In a compelling sort of way, it felt like the good road home and I liked it." She goes on to say, "My body was propped up against the shower wall and I found it odd that I was aware that I could no longer clearly discern the physical boundaries of where I began and where I ended. I sensed the composition of my being as that of a fluid rather than that of a solid. I no longer perceived myself as a whole object separate from everything. Instead, I now blended in with the space and flow around me".

While this is a valuable first-hand description of experiencing the dissolution of the "dividing line between oneself and source", as Beckwith put it, equally important is one of the primary learnings Dr. Taylor took from the experience. She describes it this way,

"In order for me to choose the chaos of recovery over the peaceful tranquility of the divine bliss that I had found in the absence of the judgement of my left mind, I had to reframe my perspective from 'Why do I have to go back' to 'Why did I get to come to this place of silence?' I realized that the blessing I had received from this experience was the knowledge that deep internal peace is accessible to anyone at any time. I believe that the experience of Nirvana exists in the consciousness of our right hemisphere, and that at any moment, we can choose to hook into that part of our brain. With this awareness, I became excited about what a difference my recovery could make in the lives of others - not just those who were recovering from a brain trauma, but everyone with a brain!".

Unfortunately, this is not a Stage where we can live continually. (Wouldn't it be nice if we could?) Fortunately, we can access and experience this Stage without having a stroke.

For me, I have had multiple experiences of being deep into nature, away from any signs of civilization, and feeling the expansive embrace of nature. It's that feeling where you know that you are a part of the web of life.

Music can also help me to dissolve any sense of separation from Source. This past Spring, I was in Europe and had two experiences of this. The first experience was being at a Franciscan monastery and participating in a Vespers service. The second was being in a Spanish synagogue and listening to a performance of classical music. The setting and the music created a sensation of my spirit, my energy, vibrating at a higher frequency, and starting to rise up.

While these examples are dependent upon something outside of myself, I and others have experienced an elimination of separateness by engaging in a variety of mindfulness practices. The practice of mindfulness frequently creates a feeling of serenity and a sense of being supported by a Loving Presence. It feels like a heightened state of meditation. It feels good.

## A Self-Help 2.0 Version of Evolutionary Growth

While Beckwith's "Four Stages of Evolutionary Growth" is a bit more practical than the concept of energy intelligence, it can still be a challenge to make it a part of your life. To bring this discussion of a transformation process closer to home, making it even more practical, let me provide you with a modified version of the Four Stages and explain how the Belief Tree model provides a step-by-step and easy to use guide for moving forward. This forward movement will help you to increasingly reach a place where you live life from a 3D perspective, from the identity of a spiritual/energetic being.

In observing my own journey and that of my clients, I would suggest that there are five stages of growth in the enlightened self-help transformational process.

**Stage One: Unaware.** This is the stage where a person is unaware/unconscious of a problem and/or growth opportunity (life's challenges aren't always negative). They are either in denial about a problem or they sense some discomfort but see themselves as victims. They believe that they are powerless and that their pain is just their lot in life. They come up with any number of rationalizations and excuses for staying stuck in their misery. They look for others to blame and take no responsibility for their own happiness. A 2D perspective on themselves and their problems is all they have ever known.

**Stage Two: Aware.** In this Stage, the pain is becoming intense enough that the person is motivated to look for a solution. They get tired of being a victim and realize that they are responsible for their own happiness.

In a positive context, this is where the person becomes aware that their life situation is another growth point. For example, they come across a book on codependency and become intellectually aware of the phenomenon and how it could be a dynamic in their life. The person is also becoming aware (hopefully) that life's challenges are a 3D puzzle and that they need to develop a 3D perspective in order to solve them.

**Stage Three: Internalize.** This is where the knowledge and increased awareness moves from the head to the heart. They see that a particular emotion or belief is impacting the quality of their life. They are open to embracing ways to grow through their current situation.

The person begins developing a connection with their Higher Power which enables them to grow with greater ease. They are ready to take responsibility for their own happiness, to help themselves, and to receive help from others.

**Stage Four: Actualize.** Here the person is actively engaged in using energy techniques to release and replace limiting emotions, beliefs, and memories with those that are more empowering, those which are highest and best for them.

This is an ongoing process which unfolds over the course of a lifetime. As a person uses energy techniques and experiences their effectiveness in reducing or eliminating items which are causing them distress, they gain confidence and comfort in using energy techniques on a wider array of items from their life.

**Stage Five: Identify.** In this stage the realization and belief that the person is fundamentally a spiritual/energetic being; that life and its challenges are a 3D phenomenon; and that they can actively tap into a Source of Loving Energy that becomes their default approach to life. They increasingly seek to live and grow through life from this expanded 3D perspective. They seek greater serenity in their life by being open to whatever is highest and best for them.

The stages I have developed are a little less conceptual than Beckwith's, but they still don't give you specifics as to what your next step could be. They are helpful in providing a larger map of the transformation process, sort of like looking at a state map.

It is my desire to give everyone a practical, step-by-step approach to self-help, to bring this discussion down to street level and provide you with a city map - one that provides you with a clearer picture of the direction you want to go. That is the purpose of the 10 Step Transformation Process which you can read about in Chapter 8.

Made in the USA
Columbia, SC
05 November 2021

48416195R00107